purely vegetarian

purely vegetarian

100 inspired recipes for everyday and special occasions

radha tabak

photographs by miki duisterhof

DEDICATION

This book is lovingly offered to my meditation teacher

CONTENTS

Stuffed poblano makhani

ON THE SIDE 79
Balsamic and maple glazed carrots
Braised carrots with tomato & thyme
Braised favas, fennel and artichokes
Fennel braised in orange juice
Green beans braised with tomato
Quinoa pilaf
Quinoa vegetable biryani
Quinoa with roasted cauliflower and olives
Ratatouille masala
Rice pilaf with carrots, currants and pine nuts
Roasted cauliflower with porcini-parmesan
   crust
Roasted maple glazed parsnips
Roasted potatoes pimentón
Sauteed kale with shiitake mushrooms
Sauteed spinach with black mission figs
Sauteed sweet corn, zucchini and bell peppers
Sweet corn fritters

SALADS 91
Arugula salad with mushrooms, pear, celery,
   walnuts and parmesan
Arugula with grapes, toasted almonds and
   manchego
Baby spinach with roasted butternut squash
   And miso dressing
Butter lettuce with avocado, mango, cucumber
   and chili-lime dressing
Cold udon noodles with broccoli, tofu and
   pickled ginger dressing
Endive, radicchio and apricot salad with goat
   cheese and almonds
Escarole with goat cheese, dates, walnuts and
   pomegranate dressing
Kale salad with pine nuts, currants and
   parmesan
Peanut sesame noodles
Quinoa with asparagus, fava, peas, mint and feta

Roasted beet salad with beet greens, orzo, feta
   and pine nuts
Watercress, jicama and orange salad with
   cilantro-lime dressing

SWEET STUFF 105
Almond, date and lemon custard tart
Apple, bread and butter pudding
Banana tart tartin with rum whipped cream
Black rice pudding with glazed bananas
Flourless orange and almond cake
Fresh ginger cakes with ginger crème anglaise
   and poached pear
Gevulde speculaas
Greta anna's plum cake
Mango and passion fruit meringue roulade
Mum's apricot nut bread
Pear, fresh ginger and date crumble
Prune flan
Rhubarb and buttermilk custard tart
Ricotta, orange and chocolate budino

INTRODUCTION

For as long as I can remember, I have had a love for cooking. I guess I must have been around age 10 when my favorite thing to do was make believe I was the host of a cooking show. I managed to regularly con my little sister to be my audience with the promise of as many chocolate crackles as she could eat! (chocolate crackle demonstrations were very popular repeats on my show).

Dad kept an organic vegetable garden and grew the most extraordinary produce. Hand picking vegetables from our garden gave me a profound respect and gratitude for nature's offerings. Grown in healthy soil, the vegetables were full of vibrance and flavor. It just doesn't get better than that.

As I grew older, I became passionate about Thai and Indian cuisines. I traveled to Thailand many times, ostensibly to vacation, but really to immerse myself in the local food: hot, sour, sweet, fragrant, and utterly delicious. India, a country where I have always felt at home, and had the good fortune to live for over 3 years. My time there proved invaluable as it gave me the opportunity to develop my palate and understanding of its complex and extraordinary cuisine.

I have been working in kitchens ever since, preparing and eating primarily vegetarian cuisine. This is my first cookbook. From the onset it felt overwhelming, but now complete, I look back and remember the wonderful moments of inspiration when I couldn't wait to try out my new ideas. I feel almost ready to start on my second book!

Most of the recipes I have developed myself. I have also included some family and traditional recipes from across the globe. There are also a few great recipes that have come across my path that I really enjoy to eat and wanted to share. Most make enough for 4-6 people; hopefully not too complicated to prepare, though some may have a few extra steps involved. There is also a section for special occasion dinners for the more experienced cook. With the growing interest in vegan cuisine, I have indicated which recipes are vegan. Almost all of my main dishes include protein in the form of dairy, eggs, beans or tofu. You won't find any recipes that include wheat gluten (seitan) or processed meat substitutes, as I never cook with them.

So here it is! 100 vegetarian recipes from my kitchen to yours. I do hope that you enjoy these recipes as much as I have enjoyed developing them for you……happy cooking!

Radha

purely vegetarian

breakfast
and brunch

swedish oatmeal pancakes with raspberry-cranberry compote

Oatmeal pancakes sound heavy, though they are surprisingly light and a fun alternative to porridge in the morning. Try these with stewed apples during autumn and winter with a dollop of yoghurt for a creamy, tangy finish.

makes approximately 12

2 cups rolled or quick-cooking oats

2 cups buttermilk

½ cup all-purpose (plain) flour

2 tablespoons white sugar

1 teaspoon baking powder

1 teaspoon baking soda (bicarbonate)

2 eggs, lightly beaten

2 ounces (60 g) unsalted butter, melted
extra butter for frying pan

3 cups fresh or frozen raspberries

2 cups fresh or frozen cranberries

½ cup white sugar

zest of one orange or lemon

Place the oats into a large bowl and add the buttermilk. Cover and let rest for 2 hours or overnight in the refrigerator. Sift the flour, sugar, baking powder and baking soda together and fold into the batter, then add the eggs and melted butter.

Heat a large frying pan over medium heat and add ½ tablespoon butter. Add ¼ cupfuls of batter into the frying pan and cook for approximately 2 minutes, or until they are golden brown underneath and bubbles form on top. Flip and cook the other side until golden. Keep cooked pancakes warm in the oven while cooking the remaining pancakes.

compote: Place the raspberries, cranberries, sugar and zest in a large saucepan. Cook over medium-low heat, stirring often, until the cranberries soften and the sauce begins to thicken. Remove from the heat and let cool. Serve warm with pancakes. Makes approximately 2 cups.

grits with cheddar, spinach, tomato and poached eggs

If you live outside the U.S., you may not be familiar with grits, a popular dish in the South. They are made from hominy corn and are very similar to polenta, which is a great substitute. Delicious topped with lashings of your favorite hot sauce!

serves 6

2 cups whole milk

4 cups water

1 cup coarse grits or polenta*

2 tablespoons unsalted butter

4 cloves garlic, minced

8 ounces (225 g) spinach leaves, tough stems removed

4 ripe tomatoes

8 ounces (225 g) sharp cheddar, grated

6 eggs

salt and pepper to taste

grits: In a heavy-bottomed saucepan, bring the milk and water to a boil. Whisking constantly, slowly pour in the grits. Return the pot to a boil, then reduce to a simmer and cook gently for 40 minutes, stirring frequently.

Meanwhile in a large frying pan, heat the butter and gently cook the garlic for 30 seconds. Increase the heat and add the spinach, stirring until it wilts. Add the tomato and cook until it begins to soften and fall apart. Remove from the heat.

Once the polenta is cooked, add the grated cheese, stirring well to fully incorporate. Then add the cooked spinach and tomato. Mix well, then season with salt and pepper and keep warm.

poached eggs: In a wide saucepan bring at least 3 inches (7.5 cm) of water to a very gentle simmer. Crack one egg into a small bowl. With a slotted spoon, create a slow whirlpool in the saucepan. Bring the egg right down to the surface of the water, and very gently slide it into the whirlpool. Gently move the egg in the direction of the whirlpool, and ensure that it doesn't fall to the bottom of the saucepan where it can stick. Cook for three minutes, then lift it out with slotted spoon and place on top of cooked polenta.

This recipe calls for the long-cooking variety of both grits and polenta, not instant.

shakshouka, pg 5

shakshouka

This recipe is essentially eggs poached in a delicious spicy tomato based sauce. Shakshouka originated in Tunisia and is very popular in Israel. I like to make this for friends when they come over for brunch. It looks really impressive when you bring it to the table. Make sure you slip an oven mitt over the handle if guests are serving themselves.

serves 4

3 tablespoons olive oil

1 onion, sliced thin

1 red or yellow bell pepper (capsicum), cored and cut into thin strips

28-ounce (800 g) can peeled whole tomatoes, crushed by hand

1 teaspoon cumin, ground

1 teaspoon coriander seed, ground

1 teaspoon, paprika

½ teaspoon freshly ground black pepper

¼ teaspoon cayenne pepper

1-2 teaspoons white sugar

8 eggs

salt to taste

1/3 cup cilantro (coriander leaves), chopped

In a large, oven-proof frying pan such as cast-iron, heat 1-2 tablespoons olive oil and sauté the onion over medium heat for 2 minutes. Add the bell pepper and sauté for 5 minutes, or until soft. Add the garlic, and sauté for another minute. Add the spices and stir for 30 seconds, then add the tomatoes and sugar. Simmer over a low heat for 15 minutes, adding water if necessary to maintain a pasta sauce consistency. Add salt to taste.

Make 6 large indentations with a spoon evenly across the surface for the eggs to nestle in. Break the eggs into indentations and season the eggs with additional salt and pepper. Cover and simmer on low until the whites are cooked but the yolks are still runny, about 5 minutes. Sprinkle with cilantro and serve with crusty toasted bread.

corn cakes with avocado and spicy tomato salsa

serves 4

4 ears sweet corn

3 scallions, finely sliced

2 jalapeño chilies, chopped finely

¼ cup cilantro (coriander leaves), chopped

1 teaspoon salt

⅓ cup milk

1 cup cheddar cheese, grated

¾ cup all-purpose (plain) flour

1 teaspoon baking powder

grapeseed oil for frying

2 ripe avocados, sliced

1 cup sour cream (optional)

cilantro (coriander leaves) to garnish

Bring water to boil in a medium sized pot. Cook the corn for 3-5 minutes, then remove from heat and allow to cool before cutting off the kernels.

In a medium-sized bowl mix together the corn, onion, jalapeño, cilantro, eggs, milk and cheddar. In a separate bowl, mix together the flour, salt and baking powder. Fold the flour into the wet ingredients; the mixture should be thick.

Heat a large non-stick frying pan over medium heat and add enough oil to cover the bottom of the frying pan. Add ½-cupfuls of corn batter and flatten into discs approximately ½ inch (1.25 cm) thick. Cook each side for approximately 2 minutes or until they are deep golden brown and spring back when you prod them with your finger. Place on a paper towel. Add more oil to frying pan and repeat. Keep finished cakes warm in the oven.

To serve, place 2-3 corn cakes on each plate and top with sliced avocado, then top with about ⅓ cup salsa, a heaped tablespoon of sour cream, and a garnish of a tablespoon of chopped cilantro.

spicy tomato salsa

¾ cup onion, chopped fine

1 clove garlic, minced

3 medium ripe tomatoes, skinned and chopped

1 small green bell pepper (capsicum), seeds removed and chopped fine

2 chipotle chilies in adobo sauce, chopped fine

1½ teaspoons salt

2 teaspoons red wine vinegar

Heat oil in a medium saucepan and gently sauté the onion and bell pepper. Continue to sauté for a few minutes or until the bell pepper begins to soften, then add garlic and sauté for 1 minute. Add the tomatoes and cook gently for a few minutes, then add the chipotle. This is spicy, so only add as much heat as you like. Add the vinegar and salt and mix well.

chickpea crepes with cilantro chutney

A dish native to Gujarat in Western India known as *besan pudla*, a thin savory pancake. This is a great protein breakfast. Eat them hot out of the pan with chutney, yoghurt or both.

makes approximately 10

1½ cups chickpea flour (besan flour*)

½ small onion, minced

¼ cup finely chopped cilantro (coriander leaves)

1 tablespoon of minced fresh ginger

1 clove garlic, minced

1-2 jalapeño chilies, minced

1 teaspoon coriander seed, ground

1 teaspoon cumin, ground

¼ teaspoon turmeric

1 teaspoon salt

⅛ teaspoon baking soda (bicarbonate)

juice of half a lemon

1½ cups water, approximately

vegetable oil

Mix all the ingredients except the baking soda and oil together in a bowl. Add enough water to make a batter the consistency of thin pancake batter. (It should be thin enough so when you pour it into the frying pan it well spread out into a thin crepe about 1/8" (1/4 cm) thickness.) Rest batter for 30 minutes before cooking. Add baking soda.

Heat about 2 teaspoons of oil in a non-stick frying pan on medium-high heat. Using a ladle, pour about ¼ cup of batter into the frying pan and spread it evenly into a 5-6 inch (12.5-15 cm) circle by lightly pushing the batter outwards in a circular motion with the back of the ladle.

When the crepe sets and turns golden on the bottom, drizzle the surface with a little oil, then flip and cook until golden. Transfer to a plate and repeat with the remaining batter. Keep warm in the oven until ready to serve.

cilantro chutney

makes 1 cup

1 bunch of cilantro

1 – 3 green chilies, minced

2 tablespoons fine chopped onion

1 tablespoon minced fresh ginger

1 clove garlic, minced

2 teaspoons sugar

½ teaspoon salt, or to taste

1 tablespoon lemon juice

¾ teaspoon cumin powder

¼ teaspoon freshly ground black pepper

2 tablespoons water, to help facilitate blending

Put everything in a blender and blend until smooth, then adjust salt, lemon and sugar to taste.

Besan flour (chickpea flour) is available in Indian food stores and health food stores.

masala scrambled egg wrap

serves 4-6

2 tablespoons olive oil

2 tablespoons butter

½ teaspoon cumin seeds

1 medium onion , fine chopped

2 teaspoons garlic, fine chopped

1 jalapeno chili, fine chopped

2 cups white button mushrooms diced ¼ inch

4 ripe roma/egg tomatoes, diced ½ inch

1 tablespoon curry powder

¼ teaspoon cayenne (optional)

1 tablespoon lemon juice

8 eggs

1 teaspoon salt

¼ cup milk

1/3 cup cilantro, fine chopped

4-6 whole wheat tortillas

¼ cup ghee or olive oil

Heat 2 tablespoons oil in a large non-stick sauté pan. Add cumin seeds and cook over a medium heat until they begin to darken. Add onions and sauté until golden brown. Add garlic, jalapeno and mushrooms and cook until mushrooms soften. Add tomatoes, curry powder, cayenne and lemon juice. Mix well and continue to cook until tomatoes soften and all liquid from tomatoes has evaporated. Remove from pan and set aside.

In a large bowl whisk eggs with milk and salt. Melt butter in the same sauté pan over a medium-high heat then add eggs. With a heat-proof spatula continue to scrape eggs from the bottom and sides of the pan until eggs are cooked but still moist. Fold in tomato mixture and cilantro then remove from heat.

Heat tortillas in a frying pan to soften, then place approximately 1 cup of scrambled egg in each tortilla while still hot, roll up and serve .

pan-fried polenta with lemon, raisins, ricotta and maple syrup

A refreshing change from pancakes. Make the polenta the day before, then all you need to do is pan fry the day you plan to serve it.

serves 4-6

2 cups milk

1¾ cups water

½ teaspoon salt

2 tablespoons white sugar

zest of one lemon

1 cup coarse polenta*

½ cup seedless golden raisins (sultanas)

3 tablespoons unsalted butter

2 tablespoons grapeseed oil

1 pound (450 g) ricotta cheese

3-4 tablespoons milk

3 tablespoons powdered (icing) sugar

1 cup maple syrup

In a medium-sized, heavy-bottomed saucepan combine the milk, water, salt, sugar and lemon zest. Bring to a boil, reduce the heat and slowly pour in the polenta in a very slow, thin stream while whisking to fully incorporate the polenta so there are no lumps. Bring to a boil then reduce heat to very low. Cook for 20 minutes, stirring every few minutes with a wooden paddle or spoon. Add the raisins and continue to cook in the same way for another 5 minutes.

Rinse a 8" x 12" (20 x 30 cm) pan or tray and shake it dry. Scrape the polenta into pan and spread evenly with a spatula. You may need to dip the spatula in hot water a few times to facilitate the spreading process. Polenta should be ½ inch (1.25 cm) thick and even.

Rest for at least 1 hour at room temperature. Cut into 12 squares. In a large, heavy frying pan heat the butter and oil over medium heat until the butter stops foaming. Add the polenta cakes and fry in batches for approximately 4 minutes on each side until golden brown. Remove and keep warm in a low oven. Add more butter to pan if necessary to complete frying all the polenta squares.

Place the ricotta in a bowl and whisk in the powdered sugar and enough milk to make it the consistency of thick yoghurt. Heat the maple syrup. Serve 2 squares of polenta on each plate with a heaped tablespoon of ricotta.
Serve and pass the maple syrup at the table.

If you make the polenta ahead and refrigerate it, bring it back to room temperature and pat it dry before pan frying.

chestnut and almond waffles with maple poached pears

A gluten-free waffle recipe, made with chestnut flour and ground almonds.

makes 6-8

poached pears:

4 bosc pears, ripe but firm

½ cup white sugar

½ cup maple syrup

4 cups (1 litre) water

zest of ½ lemon, in thick strips

2 cinnamon stick

waffles:

4 large eggs, lightly beaten

1 cup milk

4 teaspoons vanilla extract (essence)

12 ounces (340 g) unsalted butter, melted

1 tablespoon lemon juice

2 cups chestnut flour (see sources section)

⅔ cup blanched almond flour or meal

2 teaspoons pumpkin pie spice (mixed spice)

4 tablespoons white sugar

1 tablespoon + 2 teaspoons baking powder

½ teaspoon salt

pears: In a large saucepan, heat water and sugar until sugar is dissolved. Add maple syrup, lemon zest and cinnamon. Peel, quarter and core pears and add to poaching liquid.

Make sure your saucepan is big enough to comfortably fit pears so they are submerged in liquid. Simmer gently until pears are cooked through, about 15-25 minutes. Remove the pears carefully with a slotted spoon and set aside. Increase heat and reduce poaching liquid until it becomes syrupy. Remove spices and return pears to saucepan.

In a large saucepan, heat the water and sugar until sugar is dissolved. Add the maple syrup, lemon zest and cinnamon. Peel, quarter and core the pears and add them to the poaching liquid. Make sure your saucepan is big enough to comfortably fit the pears so they are submerged in liquid. Simmer gently until the pears are cooked through, about 15-25 minutes. Remove the pears carefully with a slotted spoon and set aside. Increase heat and reduce the poaching liquid until it becomes syrupy. Fish out the spices and return the pears to saucepan.

waffles: Melt the butter and let cool slightly. Whisk together the eggs, milk, vanilla extract, and butter. Whisk the chestnut and almond flour together with the pumpkin pie spice, sugar, baking powder and salt. Make a well in the center of the dry ingredients and pour in the wet ingredients. Fold together with a spatula to fully incorporate. Fold in the lemon juice. Rest for 15 minutes before cooking.

Heat a non-stick waffle iron and spray with oil. Cook waffles according to the manufacturer's instructions.

Serve the waffles with the pears and drizzle with the poaching syrup.

soups

roasted bell pepper and carrot soup

Great served either hot or chilled.

serves 4 (vegan)

1 cup onion, diced

1 tablespoon garlic, chopped finely

2 medium carrots, peeled and diced (about 1 cup)

2 large red bell peppers (capsicums)

1-2 jalapeño peppers

1 teaspoon basil, dried

1 teaspoon oregano, dried

14-ounce (400 g) can peeled or diced tomatoes

1 teaspoon smoked paprika

4 cups vegetable stock

1-2 teaspoon white sugar

salt and pepper to taste

sour cream to serve (optional)

Heat oven to 375°F (190°C) and toss the bell peppers and jalapeños in a little oil. Place on a baking tray and roast the peppers until soft, 15 minutes or so for jalapeños and 30 minutes for bell peppers. Place the peppers in a sealed container to steam for 15 minutes. Cut or tear the peppers in half and allow them to cool. Remove skins and seeds. Don't be tempted to rinse the peppers under water to remove the seeds, as this will also remove a lot of great flavor. Chop both the jalapeños and bell peppers roughly and set aside.

Heat the oil and gently sauté the onions until they soften. Add carrots, garlic, basil and oregano. Sauté for a few minutes, then cover and sweat over very low heat for 5 minutes. Add paprika, tomatoes, vegetable stock, jalapeños and bell peppers. Bring to a boil, then cover and simmer for 20 minutes. Remove from the heat and allow to cool before blending. Add sugar, salt and pepper to taste. Serve in individual bowls with a dollop of sour cream.

brazilian black bean and sweet potato soup with mango

An adaptation of a traditional Brazilian soup. The orange juice and mango are a great complement to the earthiness of the beans. Don't substitute canned beans for the dried beans in this recipe, or the outcome will be subpar.

serves 6 (vegan)

2 cups dried black beans

8 cups vegetable stock

4 tablespoons olive oil

1 pound (450 g) sweet potato, peeled, and diced into ½-inch (1.25 cm) cubes

2 cups chopped onion, in ¼-inch (0.6 cm) dice

1 green bell pepper (capsicum), in ¼-inch (0.6 cm) dice

1 stick celery, in ¼-inch (0.6 cm) dice

1 medium carrot, in ¼-inch (0.6 cm) dice

4 cloves garlic, chopped finely

2½ teaspoons cumin

¼ teaspoon cayenne

1 ½ cups fresh squeezed orange juice (juice of 3 large oranges)

salt and pepper to taste

3 ripe mangoes, in ¼-inch (0.6 cm) dice

½ cup cilantro (coriander leaves), chopped finely

Rinse the beans and cover with at least 4 cups of water. Soak for a minimum of 4 hours or overnight.

Drain the beans and place in a large saucepan with vegetable stock. Bring to a boil and cover. Reduce to a simmer and cook for about 1½ hours or until very tender.

In a large sauté pan, add 2 tablespoons of oil and sauté the sweet potato over medium heat until golden brown. Remove and set aside. In the same pan, heat 2 tablespoons of oil and sauté the onions, celery, carrot, bell pepper and garlic over medium heat until the vegetables are soft and light golden brown. Add the cumin and cayenne and sauté for another minute. Add to the beans along with the orange juice and sweet potatoes. Simmer for 10 minutes or until the sweet potatoes are tender. Add salt and freshly ground pepper to taste.

Top each serving with a few heaped tablespoons of mango and garnish with cilantro.

cannellini bean and kale soup

Soups and stews are more than just comfort food; they are dishes that combine different tastes and textures for a perfect balance. That is what makes them so satisfying to eat. I particularly like the creamy texture of the cannellini beans and how they melt into the soup so deliciously.

serves 4-6 (vegan)

1½ cups of dried cannellini beans, soaked in plenty of water for a minimim of 8 hours

2 bay leaves

3 tablespoons olive oil

1 large onion, diced finely

1 medium carrot, diced finely

1 stick celery, diced finely

6 cloves garlic, chopped finely

2 teaspoons oregano

2 teaspoons smoked paprika or pimentón

2 teaspoons sweet paprika

2 tablespoons red wine vinegar

3 ounces (90 g) tomato paste

4-5 cups vegetable stock

1 bunch curly kale, ribs removed and leaves chopped

1½-2 teaspoons salt

Drain the beans and place in a pot with 6 cups water and the bay leaves. Bring to a boil and remove any scum that comes to the surface. Cover and reduce to very low heat. Simmer for 1-1½ hours or until the beans are very tender. Remove the bay leaves and drain the beans. Reserve the cooking water.

Heat oil in a large heavy bottomed pot and sauté the onions, carrot and celery until the onions are translucent. Add the garlic and sauté for a few minutes, then add the oregano, both paprikas, vinegar, salt and tomato paste. Sauté gently for a few minutes stirring frequently. Add the reserved bean cooking water and the vegetable stock to total 8 cups of liquid. Add the kale and bring to a boil, cover, and simmer for 30 minutes. Add the beans and simmer for an additional 30 minutes.

As with all soups and stews, this tastes even better the next day. Serve with grated Parmigiano-Reggiano and crusty toasted bread.

Substitute: Great Northern or navy beans can be substituted for cannellini beans.

cauliflower and almond soup

A friend asked me if I had a cauliflower soup recipe that stood apart from the norm. I think this has now become a favorite, as he often tells me he's planning to buy a cauliflower again to make this soup!

serves 4-6 (vegan*)

2 tablespoons unsalted butter

1 medium cauliflower, quartered and sliced thinly

1 medium onion, chopped

2 cloves garlic, chopped finely

1 tablespoon coriander seed, ground

7 cups vegetable stock

½ cup ground almonds

1-2 tablespoon lemon juice

¼ teaspoon ground white pepper

salt to taste

⅓ cup cilantro (coriander leaves), chopped finely (optional)

In a wide-bottomed saucepan, heat the butter and sauté the onions over low heat until translucent. Add the garlic and coriander seed, sauté for 1 minute, then add the cauliflower. Sauté the cauliflower over medium heat, stirring often, for about 5 minutes, scraping the bottom so the coriander doesn't burn. Add ½ teaspoon of salt, mix well and cover. Reduce to very low heat and sweat the cauliflower for 10 minutes, stirring occasionally. Meanwhile, sauté the ground almonds with no oil or butter in a non-stick pan over low heat, stirring constantly, until it turns a shade darker. Remove from the pan and set aside.

Add the stock and almonds to the cauliflower and bring to a boil. Cover and simmer until the cauliflower is very tender, about 15 minutes. When cool, blend until very smooth. Add lemon juice, white pepper, cilantro and salt to taste.

*vegan: replace butter with olive oil

curried potato and leek soup

After living in India for a number of years, I was so accustomed to eating food with a lot of aromatic spices that now some dishes kind of seemed bland without it. Curry flavoring really works in this French classic.

serves 6

2 tablespoons unsalted butter

3 large leeks, washed and sliced, white and pale green parts only (5 cups)

1 tablespoon garlic, chopped finely

2 teaspoons madras curry powder

¼ teaspoon cayenne pepper

3 yellow potatoes, sliced ⅛ inch (0.3 cm) thick (about 1½ pounds or 675 g)

1½ teaspoons salt

¼ teaspoon freshly ground black pepper

6 cups vegetable stock or water

¼ cup cream (optional)

Heat the butter and gently sauté the leeks and garlic until tender. Add the curry powder and cayenne and cook for 1 minute while stirring. Add the potatoes and vegetable stock and bring to a boil. Cover and simmer gently until the potatoes are cooked, about 30 minutes. Allow to cool. Take out half of the soup and blend it until smooth. Be careful not to over-blend the soup, or the potato texture will become gluey. Return to the saucepan, add the cilantro and cream, and heat gently. Add salt and pepper to taste.

sweet corn and miso soup

A sweet corn soup, silky smooth, enhanced with white miso. This is a twist on the more traditional miso shiro,

serves 4-6 (vegan)

1 tablespoon grapeseed oil

1 cup onion, chopped finely

½ cup carrot, small dice

½ cup celery, small dice

5 dried shiitake mushrooms

3-inch (7.5 cm) piece of dried kombu seaweed

5 cups water

4 medium ears sweet corn, kernels cut from cob

⅓ cup white miso*

1 tablespoon dried wakame seaweed, soaked in ¼ cup hot water for 5 minutes.

8 ounces (225 g) silken tofu, cut into ½-inch (1.25 cm) cubes

3 scallions (spring onions), sliced finely on the diagonal, white and light green parts only

In a saucepan, heat the oil and sauté the onions until translucent. Add the water, shiitake mushrooms and kombu and bring to a boil. Simmer covered for 15 minutes or until shiitake mushrooms are tender. Remove shiitake and set aside. Add the corn and simmer for 3 minutes.

Continued on next page

Remove and discard the kombu. Allow soup to cool then place the soup in a blender along with the miso and blend until very smooth. Place a fine-meshed sieve over the saucepan and pour the soup through the sieve. Work the corn purée into the sieve with the bottom of a ladle in a circular motion until only corn skins and other solids remain in the sieve. Discard the corn skins and repeat the straining with the remaining purée. Slice shiitake mushrooms very f inely and add to soup. Drain the wakame and add to the soup. Divide the tofu between 4 small bowls and pour the soup over the tofu. Garnish with scallions and serve.

Use white, mellow white, yellow or shiro miso. sweet white miso is much too sweet to use in this recipe.

split pea and potato soup

serves 6 (vegan)

2 tablespoons olive oil

1½ cups onion, in ½-inch (1.25 cm) dice

1 cup carrot, in ½-inch (1.25 cm) dice

1 cup celery, in ½-inch (1.25 cm) dice

1 tablespoon garlic, minced

1 tablespoon fresh rosemary, chopped finely

1½ cups green split peas, rinsed and drained

1 bay leaf

8 cups vegetable stock

2-3 medium potatoes (approximately 1 pound or 450 g), in 1-inch (2.5 cm) dice

salt and pepper to taste

Heat the oil on a medium heat and sauté the onion, carrot and celery until the onions are translucent. Add the herbs and garlic and sauté for 2 minutes, then add the split peas and stock. Bring to a boil, then cover and simmer for 1 hour, stirring occasionally. Add the potatoes and continue to cook for 30 minutes. Season with salt and pepper to taste.

pasta e fagioli with porcini mushrooms

The name of this recipe literally means "pasta and beans". It's a popular soup from Italy. If you can't find tubetti pasta, macaroni works just as well. I've added porcini mushrooms for an additional flavor boost. This is a thick and hearty soup, really enjoyable during the cooler months.

serves 4-6 (vegan)

4 tablespoons unsalted butter or olive oil

1½ cups onion

1 celery stick

1 medium carrots, minced

6 cloves garlic, minced

1 tablespoon chopped fresh thyme or 1½ teaspoons dried thyme

2 bay leaves

2 ounces (60 g) tomato paste

½ ounce (15 g) dried porcini mushrooms

½ teaspoon dried chili flakes (optional)

6 cups vegetable stock

2 tablespoons red wine vinegar

1½ cups (12 ounces, 340 g) borlotti or cranberry beans soaked in water to cover for 8-12 hours

6 ounces (170 g) tubetti pasta or macaroni
salt and pepper to taste

Parmigiano-Reggiano, grated

Soak the porcini mushrooms in 1 cup boiling water for 30 minutes. Drain, reserving the soaking water.

Chop the onions, carrots, soaked mushrooms and celery roughly in a food processor, then add the garlic until chopped finely but not mushy. Heat the butter over medium heat and sauté the minced vegetables and thyme until all the liquid has evaporated and the vegetables turn a light golden color. Add the tomato paste and cook for a few minutes. Add the stock, beans, bay leaves, chili flakes, vinegar and porcini soaking liquid, being careful to leave any sandy residue from the soaking liquid behind. Bring the stock to a boil. Simmer, covered, until the beans are very tender, about 1½-2 hours, stirring occasionally, or cook in a pressure cooker for 15 -20 minutes.

Cook the pasta according to the directions on packet. Drain and add to soup.

Serve in bowls with plenty of grated Parmigiano-Reggiano cheese.

peruvian potato, cheese and avocado soup

A traditional Peruvian soup known as 'locro de papas', made with potatoes, milk, cheese and spices. You could say it's a South American chowder!

serves 4-6

2 tablespoons oil

1½ cups white onion, chopped

1 clove garlic, chopped finely

2 teaspoons cumin seeds, ground

1½ teaspoons achiote powder* (see sources)

3½ pounds (1.5 kg) baking potatoes, about 5, peeled and cut into ¾-inch (2 cm) pieces (divided)

7 cups vegetable stock or water

1 cup milk

8 ounces (225 g) mild cheddar or queso fresco, grated

2½ teaspoons salt

¾ teaspoon freshly ground black pepper

¼ teaspoon cayenne pepper

2-3 firm, ripe avocados, peeled and cut into ½-inch (1.25 cm) cubes

½ cup cilantro (coriander leaves), chopped

Heat the oil and sauté the onion until translucent. Add the garlic, cumin, achiote powder, and half the potatoes and cook over medium-high heat for 3 minutes. Add vegetable stock or water and bring to a boil, reduce the heat and simmer, partially covered, until the potatoes are tender, about 30 minutes.

Mash the potatoes into the broth. Add the remaining potatoes and simmer, partially covered, until tender. Stir in the milk and cheese and simmer for 5 minutes. Remove from the heat and add the salt, pepper, cayenne and cilantro.

Serve in bowls topped with avocado.

Achiote or annatto is a seed is commonly used in Latin American and Caribbean cuisine. Its flavor is slightly nutty, peppery and sweet. It is available both whole and powdered. If you can only source the seeds, double the quantity and sauté in oil for a few minutes, then remove the seeds and begin to sauté your onions.

peruvian potato, cheese and avocado soup pg 19

yellow split pea and spinach dhal

Typically made with toor dhal (a legume commonly used in India). Split peas make a good substitute and are easier to source.

serves 6 (vegan)

1½ cups yellow split peas (rinsed and soaked for 8 hours or overnight)

3 tablespoons grapeseed oil

1 teaspoon black mustard seeds (see sources)

1 ½ teaspoons cumin seeds

¼ teaspoon hing/asafoetida (optional)

2 cups onion, chopped finely

2 large cloves garlic, minced

1½ tablespoons fresh ginger, minced

1 tablespoon coriander seed, ground

½ teaspoon ground turmeric

½ teaspoon garam masala

¼ teaspoon cayenne pepper

1 bunch spinach, stalks removed and chopped roughly

2 teaspoon salt or to taste

3 tablespoons lemon juice

Heat oil in a large saucepan over a medium heat. Add mustard seed and when they begin to pop add the cumin seeds. Once they turn a shade darker add hing then onion. Saute onions, garlic and ginger until golden brown. Add coriander, turmeric, garam masala and cayenne pepper and sauté for 30 seconds on a low heat stirring constantly. Add tomato and cook until it breaks down (about 5 minutes.)

Add split peas and 6 ½ cups water. Bring to a boil, then cover and simmer for about 40 minutes or until completely tender. Stirring occasionally. Use a whisk to break up the split peas so it becomes creamy. Add spinach, salt and lemon juice and simmer for another 5 minutes, then serve.

red lentil, sweet potato and peanut soup with greens

A complete meal in a bowl. Top with steamed greens or my favorite, steamed broccoli.

serves 4-6

2 tablespoons olive oil

2 medium onions, small dice

1 tablespoon garlic, chopped finely

1 tablespoons ginger, chopped finely

3 tablespoons berbere (see sources)

1 cup red lentils, washed well and drained

1 pound (450 g) sweet potatoes, peeled and cut into 1-inch (2.5 cm) dice

3 ripe tomatoes, skin removed and cut into ½-inch (1.25 cm) dice

½ teaspoon turmeric

1½ teaspoons salt

6 cups water

¼ cup peanut butter

1 large head of broccoli or 1 bunch kale

In a large soup pot, heat the oil and sauté the onions over medium heat until they soften. Add the garlic and ginger and sauté for 1 minute. Add tomatoes and cook them until they begin to breakdown. Add berbere and turmeric and cook for 1 minute, while stirring. Add the remaining ingredients except the peanut butter and greens and bring to a boil. Cover and simmer for 40 minutes, stirring occasionally. Remove half of the soup and blend with the peanut butter, then return to the pot and mix well.

Cut the broccoli into florets and steam until crisp but tender, or if using greens, steam or cook in boiling salted water. Place the soup in individual bowls and top with the vegetables.

green pea and cashew soup

Cashews add a nice earthy flavor and creaminess to this lovely green soup.

serves 4 (vegan)

2 tablespoons grapeseed oil

¾ cup onion, chopped

2 cups fresh or frozen green peas

1 jalapeño chili

1 teaspoon fresh ginger, chopped finely

1 teaspoon garlic, chopped finely

⅓ cup raw cashews

1½ teaspoons curry powder

2½ cups vegetable stock

2 tablespoons chopped cilantro (coriander leaves)

¼ teaspoon ground white pepper

1 teaspoon lemon juice

In a medium saucepan heat the oil and sauté the onion on medium-low heat until translucent. Add the curry powder, cashews, ginger, garlic and jalapeño and sauté for 3 minutes.

Add the peas and vegetable stock and bring to a boil. Cover and simmer for 10 minutes. Remove from the heat and allow to cool for 30 minutes, then blend. Add the cilantro, lemon juice and salt to taste.

little bites

crostini with green pea and basil pesto

makes approximately 40

1 10-ounce (280 g) package frozen petite peas, thawed

1 garlic clove, chopped

½ cup fresh basil, chopped, plus additional small leaves for garnish

½ cup Parmigiano-Reggiano, grated

1 teaspoon salt

¼ teaspoon freshly ground black pepper

½ cup extra virgin olive oil, plus extra for the crostini

1 day-old baguette, sliced ¼ inch (0.6 cm) thick

For pea mousse: Heat the oven to 350°F (175°C). Place the peas, garlic, basil and Parmigiano-Reggiano, salt and pepper into a food processor and purée. With the processor running, slowly add ½ cup olive oil and continue to blend for one minute. Adjust the seasoning if necessary.

For crostini: Brush both sides of the bread with olive oil. Place on a tray and bake in the oven until golden and crispy, approximately 15 minutes. Watch carefully because they can easily overcook and burn. Allow to cool.
Place a heaped teaspoon of pesto on each slice of bread, top with a small basil leaf, and serve.

muhammara

A Syrian dip best served with warm pita bread. It's also great with crudites.

Pomegranate molasses gives this dip a unique flavor, but if you don't have any on-hand you can use lemon juice to taste.

makes approximately 2 cups

2 large red bell peppers (capsicums)

1 cup shelled walnuts

⅓ cup fresh breadcrumbs or Panko breadcrumbs

1 teaspoon dried red chili flakes

1 teaspoon cumin seeds, ground

1 teaspoon white sugar (optional)

¼ cup extra virgin olive oil

1½ tablespoons pomegranate molasses (see sources)

½ teaspoon salt, or to taste

Heat the oven to 375°F (190°C). Place the bell peppers on a baking tray and roast for 45 minutes. Place in a small saucepan and cover. Leave for 15 minutes, then remove skin and seeds. Do not use water to wash off seeds, as this dilutes the flavor of the roasted peppers. Place all of the ingredients in a food processor and blend until smooth.

mini samosas with cilantro and mint chutney

makes approximately 35

1 pound (450 g) yellow potatoes (2½ cups), cut into ½-inch (1.25 cm) dice

½ cup frozen peas, cooked

2 tablespoons oil

1 cup chopped onion

1 tablespoon minced fresh ginger

1 serrano, chili seeded and minced

2 teaspoons Madras curry powder

1 teaspoon salt, or to taste

2 teaspoons lemon juice

¼ cup chopped fresh cilantro (coriander leaves)

2 sheets frozen puff pastry, (each approx 10"x 9", 25 x 22.5 cm)

Place the potatoes in a saucepan and cover with water. Bring to a boil and cook until tender, then drain.
Heat the oil in large saucepan over medium-high heat and sauté the onions, ginger and jalapeño until soft and golden. Add the curry powder, salt, lemon juice, potatoes, and peas. Continue to cook for a few minutes, then remove from the heat.

Mash to break up the potatoes, mix in the chopped cilantro, and cool completely.

On a lightly floured board, roll out the pastry sheet to approximately ⅛ inch (3 mm) thick. Cut the pastry lengthwise into long strips 3 inches (7.5 cm) wide. Brush the surface of pastry lightly with water. Take handfuls of the potato mix, form it into cylinders ¾ inch (2 cm) thick, and place it along the length of pastry. Roll the pastry over the potato into a tight roll. Roll the log as if it were a rolling pin to make it more uniform. Cut across the pastry roll crosswise to form 1½-inch (4 cm) logs. Place the logs on a parchment-lined baking sheet, seam side down, allowing space for the pastry to expand while baking. Repeat with the remaining pastry. Bake in the oven at 375°F (190°C) for 20-30 minutes, until puffed and golden brown.

mint and cilantro chutney

1 bunch of cilantro (coriander), including stems, chopped roughly

1 cup fresh mint leaves

1 – 3 green chili peppers minced

2 tablespoons chopped finely onion

1 tablespoon minced fresh ginger

1 clove garlic, minced

2 teaspoons white sugar

½ teaspoon salt, or to taste

1 tablespoons lemon juice

¾ teaspoon cumin powder

¼ teaspoon freshly ground black pepper

2 tablespoons water (to help facilitate blending)

place everything in a blender and blend until very smooth.

clockwise from top: caponata stuffed eggs, pg 29

pumpernickel with roasted beets, goat cheese and pesto, pg 28

crostini with green pea and basil pesto, pg 24

walnut and mushroom pâté

Wonderful served with crackers or toasted baguette.

makes 2 cups

6 tablespoons unsalted butter

1 medium onion, cut into ½-inch dice

3 cloves garlic, minced

1 tablespoon fresh thyme, minced or 1½ teaspoon dried thyme

½ pound (225 g) cremini (Swiss brown)

½ pound (225 g) shiitake mushrooms

1 cup walnuts

½ teaspoon salt or to taste

¼ teaspoon freshly ground black pepper

¼ cup dry marsala wine or port wine

¼ cup chopped parsley

Heat oven 350F (175C)

Place walnuts on an oven tray and toast for about 10 minutes.

Heat the butter and gently sauté the onions until they turn a light golden color. Add the garlic, thyme and mushrooms. Increase the heat to medium and sauté until the mushrooms release their liquid. Add the walnuts, salt and pepper and continue to sauté until all the liquid has evaporated.

Add the port wine and cook for a few minutes. Put the mushroom mix into a food processor and process until very smooth. Add a little water if necessary to facilitate blending. Add parsley and mix well. Oil 2 small ramekins and fill with mixture then cover with plastic wrap and chill over night. Turn out onto a plate before serving.

pumpernickel with roasted beets, goat cheese and pesto

makes approximately 20

4 ounces soft goat cheese at room temperature

3 tablespoons pesto

pumpernickel bread

4 small red beets

1 tablespoon red wine vinegar

1 teaspoon honey

salt to taste

freshly ground black pepper

small basil leaves for garnish

pesto

2 cups basil leaves, packed

2 tablespoons pine nuts

¼ teaspoon salt

1 garlic clove

⅓ cup Parmigiano-Reggiano

⅛ cup olive oil

Heat oven to 350°F (175°C).
Wash beets and wrap in aluminum foil. Bake in the oven until tender when pierced with a fork, about an hour. Remove from the aluminum and allow to cool. Slip off the skins and slice into ¼-inch slices, then cut in half. In a small bowl mix together the vinegar, honey and salt, add the beets, toss gently, then set aside.

In a small food processor add the pine nuts, salt and garlic. Process until fine chopped. Add the basil and Parmigiano-Reggiano and process for a few seconds before slowly pouring in the oil to form a smooth paste.

Place the goat cheese in a small bowl and add the pesto, mixing well with the back of a spoon. Cut the pumpernickel into 1½" x 1½" squares. Set the squares out on a tray. Place a small dollop of goat cheese on top of bread, then place 2 slices of beet overlapping each other. Place a basil leaf between the beets so it is held in place. Grind black pepper on top and serve.

eggplant caponata stuffed eggs

Eggplant caponata is one of my favorite ways to eat eggplant. Makes a great appetizer filling for eggs or on toasted baguette with a shaving of Parmigiano-Reggiano. For a snack, it's wonderful on toast with melted cheese.

makes 24

5 tablespoons olive oil, divided

1 pound (450 g) eggplant*, in ¼-inch (0.6 cm) dice

1 cup onion, in ¼-inch (0.6 cm) dice

1 rib celery, cut into ¼-inch (0.6 cm) dice

1½ tablespoons tomato paste

1½ cups water

¼ cup green olives, pitted and chopped

¼ cup capers, drained

¼ cup red wine vinegar

1½ tablespoons white sugar

⅓ cup fresh basil, julienned

salt and pepper to taste

12 whole eggs

4 ounces (110 g) Parmigiano-Reggiano

In a large non-stick pan, heat 3 tablespoons of oil. Add the eggplant and sauté over medium-high heat, stirring often, until golden brown. Remove and set aside.

In the same pan, heat 2 tablespoons of oil and sauté the onions and celery over medium heat until golden brown. Add the tomato paste and cook for 1 minute, then add the water and eggplant. Simmer until the eggplant becomes very tender and liquid has reduced. Add the olives, capers, vinegar, sugar and basil. Continue to simmer until thickened. Add salt and pepper to taste.

Place the eggs into a saucepan and cover with cold water. Boil for 1 minute. Turn off the heat, cover and leave for 10 minutes. Drain the eggs and place them under cold running water until cool enough to peel. Cut the eggs in half and carefully remove the yolks from the eggs with a small spoon. Fill the egg whites with caponata.

Shave thin slices of Parmigiano-Reggiano with a vegetable peeler and top the caponata-filled eggs with a piece of shaved cheese, or garnish with a small basil leaf.

Small eggplants are the best choice, as they don't have as many seeds and tend to be less bitter. Select eggplants that are firm and shiny.

main dishes
for everyday

bubble and squeak with pan-fried tofu and onion gravy

Bubble and squeak is typically a combination of leftovers from a Sunday roast, all pan-fried together. This is the same concept without the meat. Any winter vegetable can be used: turnips, carrots, rutabagas, Brussels sprouts. I like the addition of a leafy green such as kale for a nice color contrast. Vegetables may be cooked the day before.

serves 5-6

bubble and squeak:

2 tablespoons olive oil

2 tablespoons unsalted butter

2 medium sweet potatoes

2 medium potatoes (not red-skinned variety)

¼ head cabbage

1 bunch kale, stems removed

4 cloves garlic, minced

2 tablespoons fresh thyme, chopped finely

1 tablespoons fresh rosemary, chopped finely

1 teaspoons salt, or to taste

½ teaspoon freshly ground black pepper

onion gravy:

2 tablespoons olive oil

1 tablespoon unsalted butter

3 medium onions, in ¼-inch (0.6 cm) slices

1 bay leaf

2 cups vegetable stock

1 tablespoon vegetarian Worcestershire sauce

½ teaspoon freshly ground black pepper

1 teaspoon salt

2 tablespoons all-purpose (plain) flour

tofu:

1 tablespoon olive oil

14 ounces (400 g) firm tofu, pressed (*see basic ingredients*)

4 tablespoons soy sauce

Peel and chop root vegetables roughly into approximately 1½ inch (4 cm) cubes. Chop cabbage roughly into 1-inch (2.5 cm) squares. Bring a large pot of salted water to a boil and cook the root vegetables and cabbage together for approximately 20 minutes, or until the potatoes are well cooked. Drain very well, then empty into a large bowl and mash. In a separate pot of boiling salted water, cook the kale until tender. Drain and allow to cool, then squeeze well to remove the water. Chop roughly and mix with the mashed root vegetables.

onion gravy: Heat the oil and butter in a large saucepan and sauté the onion on low heat, stirring frequently, until the onion is a deep golden brown. Sprinkle flour evenly over the top of the onions and mix well. Continue to sauté for a few minutes, then gradually add stock, mixing well as you pour the stock into pot. Add the Worcestershire sauce, bay leaf, salt and pepper. Bring to a boil, then reduce to low heat and simmer for 10 minutes. In a large non-stick frying pan, heat the oil and butter, add the garlic and thyme, and cook gently for 1 minute. Add salt and pepper, then the mashed vegetables and flatten out into a thick pancake. Cook over medium heat until a deep golden crust forms, then flip it over piece by piece and mash it back together.

Continued on next page

Continue to do this for about 20 minutes, checking every 5 minutes. Then pat it down again. When another nice brown crust forms, remove it from heat.

Slice tofu crosswise into ½-inch (1.25 cm) slices. In a separate non-stick pan, heat oil and cook the tofu over medium-high heat until it becomes golden brown, then flip over and cook the other side the same. When it is cooked, splash the tofu with soy sauce, then flip over to coat well. Remove from heat.
To assemble, place a portion of veggies on a plate, top with a slice of tofu, pour over ½ cup onion gravy, and serve.

vegan version: replace butter with oil

kale and feta pie with pine nuts and raisins

This is also very good with spinach or broccoli rabe (rapini). If using broccoli rabe, remove all the thick stems and discard. Cook the leaves and buds in boiling salted water until tender.

serves 8

4 tablespoons, olive oil

3 bunches curly kale, washed (about 1½ pounds or 675 g)

2 medium red onions, sliced

1 tablespoon chopped garlic

1 teaspoon red chili flakes

8 ounces (225 g) feta cheese crumbled

½ cup raisins (sultanas)

⅓ cup pine nuts

2 eggs, lightly beaten

olive oil

3 tablespoons unsalted butter

salt and pepper to taste

1 packet phyllo pastry, defrosted in fridge for several hours or overnight

Cut the leaves away from the kale stems and cut the stems into ¼-inch (0.6 cm) slices. Cut the leaves into ½-inch (1.25 cm) slices.

In a large pot, bring 2 cups of water to a boil. Add the cut stems and simmer until just tender (about 5 minutes) Add the leaves and continue to simmer until tender, stirring occasionally. Drain. When cool enough to handle, squeeze out as much excess water as possible and set aside.

Heat a medium sauté pan and sauté the pine nuts without any oil, stirring continually until golden brown, then remove from pan and set aside. In the same pan, heat 4 tablespoons of oil. Add the onions and sauté over low heat until golden brown, approximately 30 minutes. Add the garlic and chili flakes and sauté for 2 more minutes, then remove from the heat. Mix the chard, raisins, pine nuts, feta, onion and egg together in a large bowl. Add salt and pepper to taste. You may not need any salt at all, as feta will be quite salty.

Heat the butter and 3 tablespoons olive oil in a small saucepan until the butter has melted. Lay the phyllo open flat on the countertop and place a 9" x 13" x 2" (22.5 x 32.5 x 5 cm) baking dish on top. Cut the phyllo to fit the dish. Brush the dish with the butter/oil mix and lay a single sheet of phyllo on bottom. Brush each sheet of phyllo and lay the next sheet in until you have 6 sheets in the dish. Fill with the chard/feta mix and spread evenly. Cover with a sheet of phyllo, brush with butter, and repeat for a total of 6 sheets. *Continued on next page*

Place in oven at 375°F (190°C) and bake until golden brown, approximately 45 minutes, then serve.

cheddar and mango quesadillas with guacamole

makes 12

1 tablespoon olive oil

1 large red onion, halved and sliced thinly

2 serrano chilies, chopped finely

¼ teaspoon salt

1 tablespoon Mexican chili powder

2 semi-ripe mangoes in ¼-inch (0.6 cm) dice (2 cups)

¼ cup cilantro (coriander leaves), chopped

8 ounces (225 g) sharp cheddar, grated

12 flour tortillas

Heat the oil in a frying pan over medium heat and sauté the onion, chilies and salt until the onions are translucent. Add the chili powder and sauté for 1 minute, then remove from pan and set aside.

In a bowl, mix together the mangoes, cilantro, cheddar cheese and onions. Spray or brush oil on one side of each tortilla. Place a thin layer of filling on the side of tortilla without oil and fold in half. Heat oil in the frying pan and cook the tortillas until they are golden brown and the cheese has melted. Repeat with the remaining tortillas. Cut in half and serve with guacamole.

tofu satay burger with caramelized onions and peanut sauce, pg 55

lentil and vegetable loaf with mushroom-rosemary au jus

This is really simple to make if you have a food processor. Just toss in the carrots and celery, chop finely, and then do the same with the mushrooms. This loaf is also great served with the bell pepper gastrique (see page 7)

serves 6-8

1 cup green or brown lentils

2 tablespoons olive oil

1 large onion, chopped finely (about 2 cups)

1 medium carrot, chopped finely

1 stick celery, chopped finely

1 red bell pepper (capsicum), chopped finely

1 teaspoon dried thyme

1 teaspoon dried basil

8 ounces (225 g) mushrooms, chopped finely

1 tablespoon garlic, minced

2 eggs, lightly beaten

¼ cup ketchup (tomato sauce)

1 tablespoon soy sauce

1 cup cheddar cheese, grated

1½ cups quick-cooking oats

½ cup parsley, chopped finely

1 teaspoon salt

½ teaspoon freshly ground black pepper

Preheat oven to 350°F (175°C).

Place the lentils in a pot and cover with 4 cups water. Bring to a boil and simmer for 20-25 minutes or until the lentils are tender. Drain the lentils very well and set aside.

Meanwhile, heat the oil in a large sauté pan and sauté the onion, carrot, celery, bell pepper and garlic. Once the onion has softened, add the mushrooms, basil and thyme and continue to cook until any liquid in the pan has evaporated. Remove from heat and leave to cool. Place oatmeal in a food processor, pulse for about 10 seconds and remove.

Place the cooked lentils in a food processor and pulse a few times to break them up. This helps the loaf to bind together.

In a large bowl place the eggs, ketchup, soy sauce, lentils, sautéed vegetables, cheddar cheese, oatmeal, parsley, salt and pepper and mix well. Oil a medium-sized non-stick loaf pan. Line the bottom and the 2 long sides with parchment paper. Press the mixture into the pan, smoothing the surface. Bake for 1 hour. Allow the loaf to sit for 15 minutes before turning out and slicing. Serve with mushroom and rosemary au jus

mushroom and rosemary au jus

2 tablespoons unsalted butter

2 tablespoons olive oil

¼ cup (French) shallots, chopped finely

1 teaspoon garlic, chopped finely

1 pound (450 g) cremini (Swiss brown) mushrooms, sliced thinly

⅓ cup dry sherry

continued on next page

2 teaspoons rosemary, chopped finely

2 cups vegetable stock

1 tablespoon soy sauce

1 tablespoon cornstarch (cornflour) mixed with ¼ cup water

salt and pepper to taste

Melt butter and oil in a medium sauté pan. Sauté the shallots and garlic until softened. Add the mushrooms and sauté, stirring constantly, until the mushrooms begin to release their water. Continue to stir often until the mushroom liquid has evaporated and the mushrooms begin to brown. Add the sherry and cook until evaporated. Add the rosemary, stock and soy sauce and bring to a boil. Simmer for 5 minutes, then add cornstarch all at once, stirring at the same time so no lumps form. Simmer for a few minutes then season with salt and pepper to taste.

vegetable kootu

Also known as avial, a popular dish from Kerala, India. Don't let the simplicity of the ingredients fool you, it really has a lot of great flavor. Serve with rice to soak up the delicious coconut and gravy.

serves 6 (vegan)

1 cup fresh grated coconut (see sources)*

2-3 jalapeño chilies, or to taste

2 teaspoons cumin seeds

¼ cup onion, chopped

5 cups of mixed vegetables, cut into roughly 2 x ½-inch (5 cm x 1.25 cm) sticks (e.g., green beans, potatoes, green banana, carrots, zucchini, green peas, cauliflower, seeded cucumber, butternut squash)
1½ teaspoons salt

¼ teaspoon turmeric

2 tablespoons coconut oil

1 teaspoon black mustard seeds

12-15 fresh curry leaves (approx 1 stem) (see sources)

2-3 dried red chilies (optional)

1 tablespoon lemon juice

To make coconut purée, place the coconut, chilies, cumin seeds, onion and 1½ cups of water (or just enough to facilitate blending) in a blender. Blend into a smooth paste, approximately 3 minutes.

Place all the vegetables in a saucepan. Add 2 cups of water, the turmeric and salt. Bring to a boil, then cover and simmer until vegetables are half cooked. Add the coconut purée and continue to cook, uncovered, until the vegetables are tender.

Heat 1 tablespoon of coconut oil in a small saucepan and when hot, add mustard seeds. Once the mustard seeds begin to pop, add the dried red chilies and curry leaves and cook for 10 seconds. Add to the main dish and simmer for 2 minutes. Add lemon juice and serve.

If you are unable to get your hands on freshly grated coconut, use 1½ cups desiccated unsweetened coconut and 2 cups of HOT water to blend.

eggplant and lentil ragu

A delicious sauce, reminiscent of a Bolognese ragu. Serve with your favorite pasta or polenta and fresh grated Parmigiano-Reggiano

serves 6

¾ cup red lentils, rinsed and drained

7 tablespoons olive oil, divided

1 large eggplant (approx 1 pound or 450 g) cut in ½-inch (1.25 cm) dice

1 medium yellow onion, chopped finely

¾ cup celery, chopped finely

¾ cup carrot, chopped finely

1 tablespoon garlic, chopped finely

2 cups peeled tomatoes, crushed by hand

3 ounces tomato paste (about 3 heaped tablespoons)

1 cup vegetable stock or water

1 teaspoon oregano, dried

1 bay leaf

1 teaspoon salt

freshly ground black pepper

1 teaspoon sugar

1 pound (450 g) pasta

freshly grated Parmigiano-Reggiano cheese

Wash the lentils and place in a medium-sized saucepan with roughly 4 cups water. Bring to a boil, then reduce the heat and simmer for approximately 15 minutes or until the lentils are soft. Drain and set aside.

Heat 4 tablespoons of oil in a large non-stick pan and sauté the eggplant over medium-high heat, stirring often, until golden brown. Remove from the heat and set aside. Add the remaining 3 tablespoons of oil to a large saucepan and sauté the onion, celery and carrot over medium heat until it they begin to soften and change color. Add garlic and sauté for a few minutes. Add the eggplant, lentils and remaining ingredients, except for the pasta and Parmigiano-Reggiano. Bring to a boil, cover and reduce to a simmer. Cook until the eggplant is very tender, stirring often, about 20 minutes.

Cook the pasta until al dente, serve with the ragu and pass the Parmigiano-Reggiano

stir-fried vegetables and tofu with orange-maple glaze

A very popular dish with many of my clients over the years. The secret is to use only fresh squeezed orange juice. Sometimes I add roasted cashews for a nice crunch.

serves 4 (vegan)

4 tablespoons vegetable oil, divided

14-ounce (400 g) packet of firm tofu, pressed *(see basic ingredients)*

1 bunch scallions (spring onions)

1 small orange bell pepper (capsicum)

1 bunch asparagus

1 tablespoon ginger, chopped finely

1 tablespoon garlic, chopped finely

½ cup + 2 tablespoons freshly squeezed orange juice (approximately 2 oranges)

3 tablespoons maple syrup

1 tablespoon rice vinegar

1 tablespoon soy sauce + extra for tofu

2 teaspoons toasted sesame oil

½ teaspoon crushed red chili flakes

2 teaspoons cornstarch (cornflour)

Heat 1 tablespoon of oil in a large non-stick frying pan on medium-high heat. Fry the tofu until golden-brown. Turn over and cook on the other side. When both sides have browned, splash with a few tablespoons of soy sauce, then flip over and cook for an additional 10 seconds until the soy sauce has evaporated. Remove from the frying pan and set aside to cool. Cut each slice in half crosswise, then cut diagonally to make 4 triangles.

Wash the scallions. Cut the white and light green part of scallions into 1-inch (2.5 cm) lengths and set aside. Halve the bell pepper, remove the seeds, then slice into ¼-inch (0.6 cm) slices. Cut off the lower 2 inches (5 cm) of asparagus and cut the remaining into 1-inch (2.5 cm) lengths on the bias and set aside.

Mix together ½ cup orange juice, the maple syrup, 1 tablespoon soy sauce, sesame oil, rice vinegar and chili flakes and set aside.
Heat 1 tablespoon of vegetable oil in a large frying pan over medium-high heat. Sauté the asparagus, bell pepper and scallions, stirring constantly, until vegetables begins to brown in places. Add a few tablespoons of water to the pan and cover. Cook for 2 minutes or more for vegetables to become crisp yet tender. Remove and set aside. Add 1 tablespoon of oil to the pan and add ginger and garlic. Sauté over medium-low heat until the garlic begins to change color. Add the orange juice, mix and simmer for a few minutes.

Mix the cornstarch with 2 tablespoons of orange juice, add to the frying pan, and stir well until it thickens, about 1 minute. Add the tofu and vegetables, mixing gently so the tofu remains intact. Simmer for a few minutes, then serve.

strozzapreti with spinach sauce and sautéed mushrooms

Here is a lovely light spinach sauce for pasta. It's silky green, made without cream, and the mushrooms add a wonderful flavor and contrast. For all the kids and grown-ups out there that don't like to eat their greens, this pasta may very well convert them.

serves 6-8

sauce:

3 tablespoons unsalted butter

¾ cup (French) shallots, chopped finely

2 cloves garlic, chopped finely

½ cup basil leaves, chopped or 1½ teaspoons dried basil

1 pound (450 g) baby spinach leaves

1½ cups milk

¾ cup Parmigiano-Reggiano cheese, grated

salt and pepper to taste

mushrooms:

2 tablespoons unsalted butter

1 tablespoon olive oil

½ cup (French) shallots, halved and thin sliced

1 large clove garlic, chopped finely

1 pound (450 g) cremini (Swiss brown), shiitake or wild mushrooms

1 teaspoon fresh thyme, chopped finely

salt and pepper to taste

to finish:

1 tablespoon lemon juice

1½ pounds (675 g) strozzapreti pasta*

Parmigiano-Reggiano, grated to pass around

sauce: Melt the butter in a medium saucepan and sauté the shallots and garlic until soft. Add the spinach and basil and sauté until tender. Add the milk and bring to a boil. Simmer for a few minutes, then remove from heat. When cool, blend and return to the saucepan. Add the cheese and simmer gently until the cheese has melted. Add salt and pepper to taste.

mushrooms: Heat the butter and oil in a large non-stick frying pan and sauté shallots, garlic and thyme until shallots have softened. Add mushrooms and sauté over medium-high heat stirring frequently until mushrooms are light golden and liquid has evaporated. Season with salt and pepper to taste
To finish, cook the pasta until al dente. Drain, then add the spinach sauce and lemon juice. And mix well. Cook over medium heat for a few minutes while stirring for sauce to thicken slightly. Serve in individual bowls. Top with mushrooms and pass the cheese.

*Any type of short or curly pasta works very well with this sauce, e.g., penne, fusilli, farfalle, gemelli.

rice and beans with smoked tofu sofrito

A melee of Latin American flavors and ingredients, the rice and beans can stand on it's own and makes a great side dish. Combine that with sofrito, smoked tofu, lime and cilantro and you have a marriage made in heaven.

serves 4

rice and beans:

1 tablespoons olive oil

2 tablespoon unsalted butter

1 cup onion, finely chopped

3 cloves garlic, minced

1 teaspoon annatto, ground (see sources)

1 ½ teaspoons salt

¼ teaspoon freshly ground black pepper

2 ½ cups black beans, cooked

2 cups water

1 cup jasmine rice, washed and drained

tofu sofrito:

2 tablespoons coconut oil or olive oil

1 cup onion, small dice

1 ½ tablespoons garlic, chopped finely

1 green bell pepper (capsicum), in small dice

4 ripe medium tomatoes, skin removed

½ cup water

¼ teaspoon cayenne pepper

1 teaspoon salt

¼ teaspoon freshly ground black pepper

8 ounces (225 g) smoked tofu

¼ cup minced cilantro (coriander leaves)

3 tablespoons basil leaves, minced or 1 teaspoon dried basil

2 tablespoons fresh lime juice

rice: Heat the oil and butter in a heavy based saucepan and sauté the onion until soft. Add the garlic and cook until both onion and garlic are deep golden brown. Add the annatto, salt, pepper, rice, beans and water. Bring to a boil, cover and reduce the heat to a very low heat. Cook for 18 minutes. Turn off the heat and leave undisturbed for a minimum of 10 minutes before serving.

sofrito: Plunge the tomatoes in boiling water for 30 seconds, then place in cold water. Remove the skins, dice and set aside. Slice the short end of the block of tofu into ¼-inch (0.6 cm) planks, then cut planks in half and set aside.

In a large sauté pan, heat the oil and sauté the onions, bell peppers and garlic over medium-high heat until the onions are light golden brown. Add the tomatoes and sauté until they begin to soften. Add the water, tofu, cayenne, salt, pepper and basil and bring to a boil. Cover and simmer gently for 10 minutes, then add lime juice and cilantro and serve.

tomato and tamarind egg curry

Boiled eggs simmered in a flavorful, tomato gravy. This is wonderful served with rice or on buttered toast. Tamarind is a fruit that has a sweet-sour taste and is worth sourcing for this recipe. A tablespoon of lemon juice can be used as a substitute.

serves 4

8 eggs

3 tablespoons grapeseed oil

2 medium yellow onions, chopped finely

4 cloves garlic, chopped finely

2 teaspoons fresh ginger, chopped finely

1-2 serrano chilies, chopped finely

1 ½-2 teaspoons salt

2 tsp cumin, ground

4 tsp coriander seeds, ground

½ tsp ground turmeric

½ teaspoon ground cayenne (optional)

2 cups peeled, chopped tomatoes

2 cups water

1½ teaspoon tamarind concentrate (see sources)

1 tablespoon brown sugar

1 teaspoon garam masala

Place the eggs in a saucepan, cover with 1 inch (2.5 cm) water and bring to a boil. Boil gently for 1 minute then turn off the heat and cover with a lid. Leave for 6 minutes and rinse under cold water, then peel and set aside.

Heat the oil in a wide-bottomed sauté pan and sauté the onion over medium-low heat, stirring often until light golden brown. Add the garlic, ginger and chilies and continue to sauté for a few minutes. Add the cumin, coriander, turmeric and cayenne and sauté for 1 minute or so until the raw smell of the spices disappears. Add the tomatoes and water, scraping the bottom of the pan to incorporate any spices that may have stuck to the pan. Bring to a boil, then simmer on low heat for 20 minutes or until the sauce has thickened.

Add the tamarind, brown sugar and garam masala to the pan, mix well and let the mixture cool down for 15 minutes or so. Place the gravy in a blender and blend until very smooth, then return to the pan. Cut the eggs in half and add to the gravy, cut side up. Simmer for a few minutes until the eggs have heated through. Serve immediately.

portobello mushrooms filled with caramelized onion, spinach, tomato & mozzarella

serves 8

marinade:

1 cup olive oil

½ cup balsamic vinegar

¼ cup soy sauce

3 cloves garlic, chopped finely

8 portobello mushrooms

filling:

1 pound (450 g) baby spinach leaves

3 tablespoons olive oil

1 large sweet onion, sliced thinly

6 cloves garlic, chopped finely

4 large ripe tomatoes, skin removed and cut into ¼-inch (0.6 cm) dice

1 cup roughly chopped fresh basil

1 cup grated Parmigiano-Reggiano cheese

½ pound (225 g) fresh mozzarella, cut into ¼-inch (0.6 cm) dice

2 tablespoons unsalted butter

¾ cup panko breadcrumbs or fresh breadcrumbs

Mix the marinade ingredients together. Remove the stems from the mushrooms and wash them. Pat them dry and lay, gill side up, in a single layer in a large, oven-proof dish. Pour the marinade ingredients over the mushrooms and leave to marinate for several hours.

Cook the spinach in 2 cups boiling water until tender. Drain, cool and squeeze out as much liquid as possible. Chop roughly and set aside.

Heat oil in a large sauté pan and cook the onions over medium-low heat until golden brown. Add the garlic and sauté for a few minutes. Add the tomatoes and basil and cook until the tomatoes begin to soften, then remove from the heat.

Heat the butter in a small sauté pan and cook the bread crumbs over medium heat, stirring frequently, until golden. Place in a large bowl with the onions, spinach, tomatoes, mozzarella and ½ cup of grated Parmigiano-Reggiano.

Heat oven to 400°F (200°C). Pour off all the marinade from the mushrooms. Place the mushrooms gill side down and bake for 15 minutes. Flip the mushrooms over and fill with the tomato and cheese mix. Sprinkle with the remaining ½ cup of Parmigiano-Reggiano, and bake for 15 minutes.

kale and paneer curry

This recipe is based on saag paneer, an Indian classic. I have used kale instead of spinach, which gives this dish a vibrant green color and added nutrition. A delicious way to eat your greens. If you can't get your hands on any paneer, see basic recipes section.

serves 4 (vegan)*

paneer:

7 ounces (200 g) paneer or firm tofu, cut into ½--inch (1.25 cm) cubes

2 tablespoons grapeseed oil

½ teaspoon turmeric

¼ teaspoon cayenne, ground 1 teaspoon salt

kale:

1 pound (450 g) kale

large pinch baking soda

2 tablespoons ghee or oil, divided

2 cups onion, chopped finely

1 heaped tablespoon ginger, chopped finely

1 tablespoon garlic, minced

1 serrano chili, chopped finely

2 teaspoons coriander seed, ground

1 teaspoon cumin, ground

½ teaspoon cardamom, ground

½ teaspoon garam masala

¼ teaspoon cayenne (optional)

½ teaspoon salt, or to taste

½ cup yoghurt, beaten with a whisk

Wash kale well and pull leaves from stems. Discard stems. Bring a large pot of water to a boil, add salt and baking soda. Add kale and cook until tender. Drain and reserve 1 cup cooking liquid. Set aside.

Mix the paneer or tofu with 2 tablespoons oil, turmeric, cayenne and salt. Heat a non-stick pan and sauté the paneer over a medium heat until golden brown. Remove from the pan and set aside.

In a wider based saucepan, heat the ghee and sauté onion over a low heat until a deep golden brown. Add the garlic and ginger and sauté for a few more minutes. Add the cardamom, coriander, cumin, garam masala and cayenne and cook over low heat for 2 minutes. Add reserved kale cooking water and simmer for 5 minutes. (If you will not be using yoghurt as instructed at the end of the method, add an additional ½ cup water to the pan.) Add onions and kale to a blender and purée until very smooth.

Return the kale to the saucepan. Turn off the heat and add the yoghurt, a tablespoon at a time, mixing until completely incorporated. Repeat until all the yoghurt is added.

Add the paneer and simmer gently for 5 minutes to allow the flavors to meld. Add salt to taste and serve.

*vegan: replace paneer with tofu and omit the yoghurt

strozzapreti pasta with spinach sauce and sauteed mushrooms, pg40

spaghetti with roasted cauliflower, raisins, pine nuts and green olives

serves 4

¾ pound (340 g) spaghetti

1 small cauliflower, cut into small florets

¼ cup + 3 tablespoons extra-virgin olive oil

1 medium onion, chopped

4 tablespoons raisins (sultanas), soaked in ⅓ cup of warm water for min 20 minutes

3 tablespoons pine nuts, lightly toasted in a fry pan

3 cloves of garlic, chopped finely

A good pinch of saffron strands (soaked in 1 tablespoon warm water)

½ cup Italian green olives pitted, and chopped roughly

½ cup chopped parsley

½-1 teaspoon red chili flakes

2 tablespoons lemon juice or to taste

Salt and pepper to taste

Freshly grated pecorino cheese

Heat the oven to 400F (200°C).
Toss the cauliflower with ¼ cup olive oil and 1 teaspoon of salt and spread evenly onto a baking tray. Roast for 20 minutes.

Add 3 tablespoons of olive oil to a large frying pan and gently fry the onion until translucent. Add the garlic and chili and sauté for a few minutes more.

Add the raisins and their soaking liquid, the olives, saffron, lemon juice, salt and pepper, and mix well. Add the cauliflower. Mix well, cover, and cook gently for 3 minutes.

Cook the pasta until al dente and drain, leaving a little water clinging to the pasta, then add to the cauliflower. Mix well, then cover and cook over low heat for a couple of minutes. Add the chopped parsley and stir.

Toss the finished pasta with a little extra olive oil and serve with grated pecorino.

OPTION: Scrap the pasta altogether and serve the cauliflower as a side dish.

late summer harvest vegetable tart

This recipe can also be made with ricotta cheese to replace the sour cream, if you prefer, with an equally delicious result.

serves 8 (1-10-inch (25 cm) tart pan)

1 medium onion, diced (approximately 1½ cups)

2 large clove garlic, minced

3 tablespoons olive oil

2 ears of corn, kernels cut off

½ cup sun-dried tomatoes packed in oil, drained and chopped

12 cherry tomatoes, cut in half

1 red bell pepper (capsicum), diced

1 cup sharp cheddar cheese, grated

2 tablespoons fresh basil, chopped or ½ tablespoon dried

4 large eggs

½ cup whole milk

½ cup sour cream

1½ teaspoons salt

½ teaspoon freshly ground black pepper

10-inch (25 cm) partially baked savory tart crust (see basic recipes)

Heat oven to 350°F (175°C)
Bake the tart crust and set aside to cool.
Heat the oil in a large frying pan and sauté the onions and bell pepper until the onions are translucent. Add the garlic and corn and continue to sauté gently for 10 minutes. Remove from heat and mix in the sun-dried tomatoes and basil.

Meanwhile whisk together the eggs, sour cream, milk, salt and pepper.

Spread half the vegetable mix into the partially baked tart crust and sprinkle over half the cheese. Spread the remaining vegetables on top and then the rest of the cheese. Pour over the egg mixture and scatter cherry tomatoes on top. Bake in the oven for 1 hour or until the tart is puffed and golden.

SHORTCUT: Use a frozen pie crust and follow directions for blind-baking OR forget the crust, rub an 8 x 8 inch (20 cm x 20 cm) baking dish with butter, pour in the filling and bake until golden brown and firm to the touch.

mexican tofu fajitas

serves 4-6 (vegan)*

4 tablespoons grapeseed oil

14 ounces (400 g) firm tofu, pressed *(see basic ingredients)*

1 large onion, sliced ¼ inch (0.6 cm) thick

½ red bell pepper (capsicum), seeded and sliced ¼ inch (0.6 cm) thick

½ yellow bell pepper (capsicum), seeded and sliced ¼ inch (0.6 cm) thick

12 flour tortillas

1½ cups sour cream

2 large ripe tomatoes, chopped

1 cup cilantro (coriander leaves), chopped

fajita sauce

3 tablespoons lime juice

⅓ cup water

3 cloves garlic, minced

2 teaspoons Mexican chili powder (see sources)

1 teaspoon cumin powder

¾ teaspoon freshly ground black pepper

¾ teaspoon salt

1½ tablespoons vegetarian Worcestershire sauce

1½ teaspoons smoked paprika

1 ½ tablespoons brown sugar

Mix the sauce ingredients together and set aside.

Rinse and dry the tofu. Slice crosswise into ¼ inch (0.6 cm) slices. Heat a large non-stick pan and add 2 tablespoons of oil, then pan-fry the tofu on high heat until golden brown and flip. Remove from the pan and set aside. Repeat with the remaining tofu and set aside. Then cut the tofu slices into 4 pieces crosswise.

In a large sauté pan, add 2 tablespoons of oil and sauté the onions and bell peppers over high heat, stirring often, until the onions and bell peppers have softened and are blackened in places. (You may want to cook onions and bell peppers separately so you don't overcrowd the pan.) Add the tofu and sauce to pan and cook for 3-5 minutes, stirring gently, until most of the liquid has evaporated.

Wrap the tortillas in aluminum foil and heat in a moderate oven for 10 minutes. Fill the warmed tortillas with tofu, sour cream, chopped tomatoes and cilantro.

vegan: use vegan sour cream

black pepper tofu and green beans

An adaptation of a recipe by Yottam Ottolenghi. I've added vegetables to give a fresh crisp texture and color to this unusually delicious recipe. It seems like a lot of pepper but it has the most incredible flavor.

serves 4 (vegan*)

2 tablespoons grapeseed oil + extra for frying tofu

½ pound (225 g) green beans, cut into 1-inch (2.5 cm) lengths

1 large red bell pepper (capsicum), seeded and cut into ¼-inch (0.6 cm) sticks

½ teaspoon salt

14-ounce (400 g) packet firm tofu, pressed *(see basic ingredients)* and cut into ¾ inch (1.8 cm) cubes

1 cup cornstarch (cornflour)

3 tablespoons unsalted butter

1 cup sliced (French) shallots

2 fresh mild red chilies, thin sliced

1½ tablespoon garlic, chopped finely

1½ tablespoon ginger, chopped finely

2 tablespoons Ketchap Manis/sweet soy sauce (see sources)

2 tablespoons soy sauce

1 teaspoon molasses

2 tablespoons brown sugar

2 tablespoons coarsely cracked black pepper

Heat oil in a large frying pan. Over high heat, sauté the green beans and bell pepper until dark brown in places. Add the salt and ¼ cup water, cover and reduce to medium-low heat. Cook for 3-4 minutes or until green beans are crisp-tender. Remove from pan, including the liquid, and set aside.

Wipe the pan dry and heat enough oil to cover the surface. Toss the tofu in the cornstarch and shake off the excess. Add to the hot oil and cook over medium heat in batches with space between them so they don't stick to each other. Fry until they are golden all over and have a thin crust. Once cooked, transfer the tofu onto a paper towel.

Wipe out the pan and add the butter, shallots, chilies, garlic and ginger. Sauté on low heat for about 15 minutes, stirring occasionally, until the ingredients have turned shiny and are totally soft. Next add the soy sauces and sugar and stir, then add the cracked black pepper.

Add the green beans, bell pepper and tofu and mix well. Sauté for a few minutes for flavors to come together.

*vegan: replace the butter with 2 tablespoons grapeseed oil

butternut squash and ricotta galette with sage butter

A galette is a free-form tart that doesn't require blind baking. Just roll out your pastry, place the filling on top, fold over the edges to form a border and bake!

Pastry:

2 cups all-purpose (plain) flour

1 teaspoon salt

1 teaspoon sugar

6 oz (170 g) unsalted butter, cut into ½-inch dice

¼ cup ice water

1 egg

filling:

1 small butternut squash, about 1½ Lbs (700 g)

6 ounces (170 g, about 1 cup) ricotta cheese, drained

1 cup Parmigiano-Reggiano cheese, grated

1 teaspoon salt (divided)

2 teaspoons olive oil

freshly ground black pepper

2 ounces (60 g) unsalted butter

12 fresh sage leaves (approx)

1 tablespoon brown sugar

pastry: In a food processor, add the flour, salt, sugar and butter, and process until butter is mostly, but not fully, incorporated. You want to still see pea-sized chunks of butter. Whisk together the ice water and egg and add while the machine is running. When the pastry begins to come together, turn it out onto a flat surface. Knead gently a few times, just to bring it all together, then flatten into a disk about ½ inch (12.5 mm) thick. Wrap in plastic wrap and refrigerate for about an hour.

filling: Peel, quarter and slice the butternut squash a bare ¼ inch (6 mm) thick and set aside. Mix together the ricotta, Parmigiano-Reggiano and ½ teaspoon salt and set aside. In a large bowl, mix the butternut squash and olive oil. Mix in ½ teaspoon salt and some freshly ground black pepper.

Roll out the pastry on a floured surface to a ⅛-inch thick disc. Transfer to a parchment-lined cookie sheet tray. Spread the ricotta mix evenly over the surface, leaving a 2 inch (5 cm) border. Starting from the outside in, tightly shingle or layer the butternut squash over the ricotta in a circular fashion. Fold the border of the pastry over the filling.

Melt the butter, add the sage leaves and simmer for 2 minutes. Drizzle the butter over the surface of the butternut squash, leaving the sage leaves behind (save them for garnish later). Sprinkle the squash with the brown sugar. Bake at 400°F (200°C) for 45-50 minutes, or until the butternut squash is tender and the pastry is golden brown and garnish with reserved sage leaves.

butternut squash and ricotta galette with sage butter, pg 50

malaysian-style vegetable and tofu curry

Here I have used sweet potato and green beans, though this recipe is very flexible. You can really use any vegetable you have on hand, though a root vegetable does add a nice texture. Chickpeas may be substituted for tofu. Serve with jasmine rice or your favorite grain.

serves 4-6 (vegan)

12 whole cashews, raw or roasted

4 large (French) shallots, chopped

5 cloves garlic, chopped

2 tablespoons ginger, chopped

3 sticks lemongrass

4 tablespoons grapeseed oil (divided)

2 tablespoons Malaysian or Madras curry powder

½ teaspoon turmeric

1 teaspoon salt

¼ teaspoon cayenne (optional)

14 ounces (400 ml) coconut milk

2 tablespoons soy sauce

2 tablespoons brown sugar

1 cinnamon stick

2 star anise

8 ounces (225 g) sweet potato, cut into 1½-inch (3.75 cm) chunks

8 ounces (225 g) green beans, cut to 1½ inches (3.75 cm)

8 ounces (225 g) eggplant, cut into 1 inch (2.5 cm) chunks

14-ounce (400 g) packet soft or firm (not silken) tofu, cut into ¾-inch (1.8 cm) slices.

1 tablespoon lemon juice

Place the cashews and ½ cup water in a small saucepan and bring to a boil. Turn off heat and leave the cashews to soften for at least 30 minutes.

Remove the outer layer of lemongrass, slice off the hard nub at the bottom then slice the bottom 6 inches (15 cm), discarding the green stalk. Place the cashews and soaking water in blender along with the shallots, garlic, ginger and lemongrass. Blend until *very* smooth.

Heat 3 tablespoons of oil in a heavy-bottomed saucepan over medium heat. Add the blended paste and bring to a boil, then reduce heat and simmer, stirring often, until the paste begins to dry out and catch on the bottom of the saucepan. Add the curry powder, turmeric, salt and cayenne and continue to cook for another minute or so. Gradually add coconut milk, whisking to remove any lumps that may form.

Add 2 cups of water, the soy sauce, sugar, cinnamon and star anise. Bring to a boil, and then add the sweet potato and eggplant. Cover, reduce to a simmer and cook until vegetables are tender.

moroccan braised vegetables with chickpeas and dates

serves 4 (vegan)

2 tablespoons olive oil

2 tablespoons unsalted butter

1 medium red onion, sliced ¼ inch (0.6 cm) thick

1 small eggplant (8 ounces, 225 g), cut into ½ inch x 1½ inch (1.25 cm x 3.75 cm) sticks

4 medium carrots, peeled and cut into ½ inch x 1½ inch (1.25 cm x 3.75 cm) sticks

1 tablespoon garlic, chopped finely

1 teaspoon dried, ground ginger

½ teaspoon turmeric

2 cinnamon sticks

1 teaspoon ground coriander seed

½ teaspoon freshly ground black pepper

¼ teaspoon cayenne (or to taste)

2½ cups vegetable stock

5 sprigs parsley

1- 1½ teaspoons salt

1½ cups chickpeas, cooked

12 small dates, seed removed and halved

1 tablespoon lemon juice

3 tablespoons cilantro (coriander leaves), chopped roughly

Mix together the dried ginger, turmeric, cinnamon stick, coriander seed, black pepper, 1 teaspoon of salt and cayenne. Tie the parsley together with a piece of string like you would a bouquet garni.

Add the oil and butter to a large sauté pan over medium heat. Add the garlic and onion and sauté until onion softens. Add the eggplant and carrots and sauté for approximately 5 minutes, stirring often. Add the spices, mix well and continue to stir for about 30 seconds so the spices don't burn.

Add the vegetable stock and parsley and bring to a boil, cover and simmer for 10 minutes. Add the dates, lemon juice and chickpeas and continue to simmer covered until vegetables are very tender. Remove the parsley and cinnamon sticks and discard. Garnish with chopped cilantro and serve with quinoa, couscous or rice.

portobello mushroom burgers with peperonata, arugula pesto and mozzarella

serves 6

6 burger buns, toasted

1 pound (450 g) fresh mozzarella, sliced ½ inch (1.25 cm) thick

mushrooms:

6 portobello mushrooms

¾ cup olive oil

⅓ cup balsamic vinegar

3 tablespoons soy sauce

2 cloves garlic, chopped finely

peperonata:

4 tablespoons olive oil

1 medium onion, sliced thinly

4 cloves garlic, chopped finely

4 bell peppers (capsicums), a combination of red, yellow or orange

1 teaspoon salt

4 roma tomatoes, diced

⅓ cup water

1 tablespoon red wine vinegar

arugula pesto:

4 packed cups arugula (approximately 4 ounces or 110 g)

⅓ cup extra-virgin olive oil

½ cup finely grated Parmigiano-Reggiano

⅓ cup pine nuts

2 teaspoons lemon juice

2 teaspoons lemon zest

1 clove garlic, chopped

Kosher salt and freshly ground black pepper, to taste

mushrooms: Mix together the vinegar, soy sauce and garlic, then slowly whisk in the olive oil. Remove the stems from the mushrooms and wash to remove any dirt. Pat dry and lay in a single layer in a large oven-proof dish, gills facing upward. Pour over the marinade and leave for several hours or overnight. Cook mushrooms on a barbecue grill until tender or bake in an oven at 400°F (200°C) and cook gill side down for 15-20 minutes.

peperonata: Remove the seeds from the bell peppers and cut into ¼-inch (0.6 cm) slices. Heat oil in a large sauté pan and sauté the onions, bell peppers and garlic for a few minutes. Add the salt, tomatoes and water and bring to a boil, then cover partially. Cook on low heat until the bell peppers are tender, about 45 minutes. Add the vinegar and salt and pepper to taste.

pesto: Place all the pesto ingredients except the oil in a food processor until finely chopped. Slowly pour in the oil while the machine is on. Season with salt and pepper to taste.

to finish: Turn the mushrooms gill side up, fill with a few heaped tablespoons of peperonata, and top with mozzarella. Return to the oven or grill and continue to cook until heated through. Spread a heaped tablespoon of pesto on both sides of a toasted burger bun before placing a mushroom on the bun, then serve.

tofu satay burger with caramelized onions and peanut sauce

This burger has been tested on hard-core meat eaters with a big thumbs-up!
Marinating the tofu and making the sauce the day before cuts the preparation time down for the day you serve this dish.

serves 5-6 (vegan)

tofu marinade:

¼ cup (French) shallots, chopped

3 cloves garlic

¼ teaspoon cayenne pepper

1 thumb-sized piece of ginger, chopped

2 tablespoons ground coriander seed

2 teaspoons ground cumin

6 tablespoons soy sauce

1 tablespoon molasses

3 tablespoons brown sugar

sauce:

2 tablespoons grapeseed oil

½ cup (French) shallots, chopped finely

5 cloves garlic, chopped finely

½ cup crunchy peanut butter

1 tablespoon Sriracha or sambal oelek

2 tablespoons brown sugar

3 tablespoons soy sauce

¾ cup water

2 teaspoons lemon juice

burger:

4 tablespoons grapeseed oil (divided)

3 large onions, sliced thinly

½ teaspoon salt

5 lettuce leaves

2 ripe tomatoes, sliced

5 eggs (optional)

5 burger buns

tofu: Place the marinade ingredients in a food processor and blend until smooth. Drain the tofu and pat dry, then cut into 6 slices. Lay the tofu in a single layer in an ovenproof dish and pour over half of the marinade, coating the tofu well. Marinate for at least one hour. Bake at 375°F (190°C) for 45 minutes, turning occasionally to bake the tofu evenly.
The remaining marinade can be frozen for another time.

burger: Heat 3 tablespoons grapeseed oil and the onions in a large frying pan over high heat, stirring constantly until the onions begin to char or blacken. Add ½ teaspoon salt and reduce heat to medium-low, stirring often, until onions become very soft and deep golden brown. Remove from heat and keep warm.

sauce: While the onions are cooking, heat 2 tablespoons of oil in a large sauté pan and gently sauté the shallots until golden brown. Add the garlic and continue to sauté for a few minutes. Add the peanut butter, chili, sugar, soy sauce, salt, water and lemon juice. Mix well and simmer for 5 minutes. Remove from heat and set aside.

to finish: Heat 1 tablespoon of oil in a non-stick pan. Fry eggs however you like them and season with salt and pepper. Keep warm.

Continued on next page

Toast the burger buns and place a heaped tablespoon of peanut sauce on each side. On the base of the bun, place a piece of tofu, an egg, onion, tomato, and lettuce. Add an extra squirt of sriracha (optional) then cover with the bun top and serve.

winter vegetable and miso stew

serves 4 (vegan*)

10 dried shiitake mushrooms

3 inch (7.5 cm) piece kombu

4 cups water

1 medium onion, chopped finely

½ bunch scallions (spring onions), sliced thinly

2 tablespoons ginger, cut into thin matchsticks

2 large clove garlic, sliced thinly

2 cups sweet potato, cut into 1-inch (2.5 cm) chunks

1 medium eggplant or 3-4 Asian eggplants, cut into ½-inch (1.25 cm) dice
(about ½ pound or 225 g)

2 tablespoons unsalted butter

2 tablespoons tamari or soy sauce

2 tablespoons mirin

1 teaspoon white sugar

3 cups kale, ribs removed and rough chopped (packed)

1 heaped tablespoon tahini (sesame paste)

¼ cup white miso, or more

In a medium sized saucepan, bring 4 cups water to a boil. Add the dried shiitake mushrooms and kombu. Cover and remove from heat. Leave for 30 minutes, then remove the mushrooms and kombu, reserving the mushroom broth. Remove the stems from mushrooms and discard. Quarter the mushroom caps and return to the pot of mushroom broth.
In a large wide saucepan over medium-high heat, add the butter and sauté the onions, scallions, garlic and ginger.

Add the mushroom broth, leaving any residue that may have settled on the bottom of the vessel behind. Add the soy sauce, mirin, sugar, sweet potato and eggplant. Bring to a boil, cover and simmer gently for 10 minutes. Add the kale and simmer until the kale is tender, about 5 minutes. Place the miso and tahini in a small bowl. Remove 1 cup of broth from the saucepan, add it to the miso, and whisk until smooth. Return the miso liquid to pot, mix well and serve.

vegan: replace butter with grapeseed oil

tofu alla cacciatora

Tofu cooked in the style of this well-known Italian dish. I've added mushrooms and olives which isn't typical, but I like the added flavor that they give. Serve with your favorite grain, or pasta.

serves 6 (vegan)

½ cup grapeseed oil

21 ounces (600 g) firm tofu (approximately 1½ packets, pressed (see recipe ingredients)

1 cup all-purpose (plain) flour, approximately

3 tablespoons, olive oil

2 cups cremini (Swiss brown) mushrooms, quartered

1 small onion, diced

1 stalk celery, sliced thinly

1 medium carrot, quartered lengthwise and sliced thinly

1 red bell pepper (capsicum), diced

2 teaspoons rosemary, minced

2 cloves garlic, minced

1 bay leaf

⅔ cup dry white wine

1 28-ounce (800 g) can whole peeled tomatoes, crushed by hand

½ cup vegetable stock

12 pitted green Italian olives

salt and freshly ground pepper to taste

1 tablespoon finely chopped parsley

Cut the tofu into approximately 1 inch (2.5 cm) cubes. Place on a paper towel and pat dry. Season with salt and pepper, then toss the tofu in flour and shake off the excess.

Heat the grapeseed oil in a large frying pan. Cook the tofu in batches so it doesn't stew in the pan. Fry, turning the pieces around as you go, until they are golden all over and have a thin crust. As they are cooked, transfer them onto paper towels.

In a large sauté pan, heat the olive oil, add the onion, celery, carrot, red bell pepper, mushrooms, rosemary and garlic, and sauté until golden brown, about 8-10 minutes. Add the wine and cook until reduced by half. Add the tomatoes, olives and stock and simmer, covered, for about 20 minutes. Add the tofu and simmer uncovered for 10 minutes. Add the parsley and salt and pepper to taste and

vegetable and cannellini goulash with parsley dumplings, pg 60

tofu and vegetable bourguignon pie

My husband, who isn't a vegetarian, loves this dish. It's big on flavor and very satisfying to eat. There are a few ways you can serve this, either by making one big pie or individual pies in ramekins. Or forgo the pastry all together and serve with mashed potatoes and sautéed leafy greens. It's all good!

serves 4-6

½ ounce (15 g) dried porcini mushrooms

5 tablespoons olive oil (divided)

7 ounces (200 g) firm tofu, cut into ½ inch cubes

1 tablespoon soy sauce

1 onion, sliced thinly

3 medium carrots, cut ½ inch (1.25 cm) on the diagonal

1 stick celery, cut into ½-inch (1.25 cm) slices

2 cloves garlic, chopped finely

1 teaspoon fresh thyme, chopped finely

1 bay leaf

1 teaspoon rosemary, chopped finely

1 heaped tablespoon tomato paste

1½ cups red wine

½ cup water

1 heaped teaspoon vegetable bouillon

8 ounces (225 g) cremini (Swiss brown) mushrooms, quartered

1 cup pearl onions, frozen

2 tablespoons unsalted butter, at room temperature

1 ½ tablespoons all-purpose (plain) flour

1 sheet puff pastry, defrosted

1 egg

Soak the porcini mushrooms in a bowl with 1 cup of boiling water and set aside for 30 minutes or more.

Heat 1 tablespoon of oil in a non-stick frying pan and sauté the mushrooms over medium-high heat, stirring often until they begin to brown. Remove and set aside. Heat an additional 2 tablespoons of oil and sauté the tofu cubes using a heat-proof spatula to move them around gently so they don't break. When golden, splash them with soy sauce and cook until the liquid has evaporated.

Heat 2 tablespoons of oil in a large saucepan over medium heat and sauté the onion, carrot and celery, stirring often, until light golden brown. Add the garlic, thyme, bay leaf, rosemary and tomato paste. Sauté for a minute, then add wine, water and bouillon. Strain the porcini mushrooms, reserving the soaking liquid. Chop the porcini finely and add to the pot along with the soaking liquid, pouring slowly to keep any sandy sediment that may have settled on the bottom aside. Bring to a boil, then cover and simmer for 20 minutes.

Add the tofu, mushrooms and pearl onions and simmer, partially uncovered, for 10 minutes. Make a beurre manié by mixing together the butter and flour. Add ¼ cup or so of gravy to the beurre manié and mix until smooth. Return to the pot, mix well and simmer for a few minutes while it thickens. Remove from the heat and pour into a deep pie dish and leave to cool completely.

Continued on next page

Heat oven 375°F (190°C). Roll out the pastry to a generous ⅛-inch (0.3 cm) thickness on a lightly floured surface. Using a dinner plate as a guide, cut a circle of pastry big enough so it will drape about ½ inch (1.25 cm) over the sides of pie dish. In a small bowl, lightly beat an egg. Using a pastry brush, brush the circumference of the pastry with egg. When the filling is room temperature, drape the pastry egg side down over the pie filling and press the edges around the rim. Using the tip of a sharp knife, cut a few decorative vent holes in the top of the pastry circle, and then brush the surface of the pastry with egg.

Place the pie in the center of the oven and bake until puffed and golden, about 20-25 minutes. Serve immediately.

vegetable and cannellini bean goulash with parsley dumplings

A great winter meal, and the fluffy steamed dumplings are a treat. Use a fresh container of Hungarian paprika if you can, as it does make a difference to the overall taste.

serves 4-6 (vegan*)

1 cup dried cannellini beans, soaked overnight*

4 tablespoons olive oil

1 pound (450 g) cremini (Swiss brown) mushrooms, stems removed and sliced ¼ inch (0.6 cm) thick

1 large onion, in ½-inch (1.25 cm) dice

1 green bell pepper (capsicum), seeded and cut into ½-inch (1.25 cm) dice

1 medium carrot, peeled and cut into ½-inch (1.25 cm) dice

1 tablespoon garlic, chopped finely

4 tablespoons tomato paste

2 teaspoons fresh thyme, chopped finely or 1 teaspoon dried

2 teaspoons marjoram, dried

1 teaspoon caraway seeds

2 tablespoons sweet Hungarian paprika

½ teaspoon cayenne (optional)

5 cups vegetable stock

12 ounces (340 g) cabbage, in ½-inch (1.25 cm) dice, approximately 4 cups

2 teaspoons brown sugar

1 tablespoon red wine vinegar

1 bay leaf

⅓ cup parsley, chopped finely

salt and pepper to taste

dumplings:

1 cup all-purpose (plain) flour

2 teaspoons baking powder

½ teaspoon salt

1 tablespoons unsalted butter, melted

½ cup + 2 tablespoons milk

2-3 tablespoons parsley, chopped finely

goulash: Drain the beans and cook in at least 4 cups water until tender. Drain and set aside. Heat 2 tablespoons olive oil in a large frying pan. Sauté the mushrooms on high heat until they begin to brown and all the liquid has evaporated. Remove from pan and set aside.

Continued on next page

Add 2 tablespoons oil to a large wide saucepan, then add the onions, carrots and bell pepper. Sauté over medium-high heat until onions are translucent and vegetables begin to brown. Add the garlic and sauté for 2 minutes. Add the tomato paste, thyme, marjoram, caraway, paprika and cayenne. Continue to sauté for a minute, then add the stock, cabbage, cooked beans, vinegar, sugar and bay leaves. Bring to a boil, cover and simmer for 15 minutes. Add the parsley and mushrooms and turn off the heat.

dumplings: It is important to use exact measurements. Sift together the flour, baking powder and salt. Melt the butter and add to the milk. Combine the wet and dry ingredients and mix until just combined. Bring the stew back up to a slow simmer. Drop the dumpling batter by (heaping) teaspoonfuls into the simmering stew. Cover and simmer for 15 minutes. Once you have covered the pan, ***do not uncover*** while the dumplings are cooking! In order for them to be light and fluffy, they must steam. After 15 minutes, test the dumplings with a toothpick. If the toothpick comes out clean, the dumplings are done. Serve immediately.

vegan: replace butter with oil and milk with soy milk

1 cup dried beans = 3 cups cooked

fancy fare

for special occasions

radicchio and goat cheese crespelle with besciamella

Crepes filled with sautéed onion, radicchio and goat cheese with a light Parmigiano-Reggiano sauce. The combination is surprisingly delicious. A crisp green salad is a great accompaniment.

serves 4

crespelle:

 1 cup all-purpose (plain) flour

¼ teaspoon salt

⅔ cup cold milk

⅔ cup cold water

5 tablespoons unsalted butter, divided

3 large eggs

filling:

3 tablespoons olive oil

1½ cup red onion, chopped finely

1 head radicchio, chopped into ½-inch dice

1 teaspoon fresh rosemary, chopped finely

8 ounces (225 g) soft goat cheese

2 tablespoons balsamic vinegar

¼ cup parsley, chopped finely

besciamella:

 4 tablespoons unsalted butter

3 tablespoons all-purpose (plain) flour

½ teaspoon salt

2 cups milk

¾ cup Parmigiano-Reggiano, fresh grated

3 tablespoons parsley, chopped finely

crespelle: Mix the flour, salt, water, milk and 3 tablespoons melted butter together in a blender until smooth. Refrigerate for 30 minutes.

Heat a 8" or 10" (20 or 25 cm) non-stick frying pan over medium heat. Brush with melted butter.
Pour about 3 tablespoons of batter into the center of the pan and then tilt the pan in all directions to cover the bottom evenly. Cook about 1 minute, or until browned on the bottom. Turn and cook briefly on the other side. Stack the cooked crespelle on a plate until ready to use

filling: Heat the olive oil in a sauté pan and sauté the onions until soft. Add the radicchio and rosemary and continue to cook for 5 minutes. Turn into a large bowl and allow to cool. Add the parsley, balsamic vinegar and goat cheese and mix well. Spread 2-3 tablespoons of filling onto one quarter of each crespella, then fold the crespella over the filling and then in half again so it becomes a quarter circle. Butter the bottom of a large oven-proof dish and shingle the filled crespelle into the dish.

besciamella: Melt the butter in a small saucepan and add the flour. Gently cook, stirring frequently, for 5 minutes. Add the milk and whisk together. Increase the heat and continue to stir as it begins to thicken, to ensure lumps don't develop. Simmer for 5 minutes, then add half a cup of grated Parmigiano-Reggiano and salt and pepper to taste.

Pour the besciamella evenly over the crespelle and sprinkle with the remaining Parmigiano-Reggiano. Place the dish in a 375°F (190°C) oven and bake for 15 minutes.

Garnish with chopped parsley and serve.

sesame-crusted tofu with sweet potato purée, stir-fried bok choy, and hoisin-ginger sauce

serves 4 (vegan)

sesame tofu:

14-ounce (400 g) packet firm tofu, pressed *(see basic ingredients)*

¼ cup + 1 teaspoon soy sauce

1 egg

1 cup all-purpose (plain) flour

1 cup sesame seeds

oil for frying

sweet potato purée:

3 pounds (1.35 kg) sweet potato, peeled and cut into large chunks

2 tablespoons oil

½ cup (French) shallots, chopped finely

2 tablespoons fresh ginger, chopped finely

½ cup coconut milk

1½ teaspoons salt

¼ teaspoon white pepper

hoisin-ginger sauce:

2 tablespoons grapeseed oil

⅓ cup (French) shallots, chopped finely

1½ tablespoons fresh ginger, chopped finely

2 cloves garlic, chopped finely

2 tablespoons dry sherry

2 tablespoons hoisin sauce

3 tablespoons sweet soy sauce or dark soy sauce

1 tablespoon brown sugar

¼ teaspoon five spice powder

½ teaspoon red chili flakes

1 tablespoon rice wine vinegar

½ cup water

1 teaspoon cornstarch (cornflour)

1 tablespoon cold water

bok choy:

2 tablespoons oil

1½ pounds (675 g) baby bok choy

3 cloves garlic, peeled and thin sliced

1 tablespoon soy sauce

1 teaspoon salt

3 tablespoons mirin

sesame tofu: Cut the tofu lengthwise into 3 slices, then cut the slices in half crosswise. Place in a single layer in a square cake tin or something similar. Pour over ¼ cup of soy sauce and leave for 30 minutes, flipping the tofu over every 10 minutes. Remove from the tin and pat dry. Place the flour on a plate. Lightly beat the egg in a bowl with 1 teaspoon soy sauce and place the sesame seeds on another large plate. Lightly coat the tofu in flour, then dip in the egg, shaking off the excess. Then press into sesame seeds, repeating with remaining tofu. Refrigerate until ready to use.

Continued on next page

sweet potato purée: Boil the sweet potatoes in water until very tender, then drain well. Heat the oil and sauté the shallots and ginger until very soft (about 4 minutes). Add the coconut milk and salt and simmer for about 3 minutes. Add the sweet potatoes and mash well. To make it very smooth, you may want to use an electric hand mixer. Adjust the seasoning, then cover and set aside.

sauce: Heat the oil in a small saucepan and sauté the shallots, ginger and garlic until soft. Add the sherry, soy sauce, hoisin sauce, sugar, chili flakes, five spice powder, water and rice wine vinegar and bring to a boil. Simmer for 5 minutes, then mix the cornstarch with cold water and add to sauce while stirring. Simmer for 2 minutes, then set aside and keep warm.

bok choy: cut bok choy in half and wash thoroughly, drain and set aside. In a large non-stick pan, heat the oil over medium heat and sauté the garlic for a few minutes or until light golden. Add the bok choy and increase the heat to high. Using tongs, continue to flip the bok choy until it begins to soften. Add the salt, soy sauce and mirin. Continue to flip until crisp tender. Set aside and keep warm.

to finish: Cover the surface of a large frying pan with ¼ inch (0.6 cm) of oil and heat over medium heat. When hot but not smoking, add the tofu and cook until golden brown, then drain on paper towels. On the center of each plate, mound 1 heaped cup of sweet potato purée, then surround the purée with bok choy. Place a piece of tofu in the center of the purée, then drizzle the tofu and bok choy with a little less than ¼ cup of sauce and serve.

*vegan: omit flour and egg preparation and just dust tofu all over with cornstarch. Leave for 5 minutes until the surface of tofu becomes sticky, then press tofu. into sesame seeds.

sesame crusted tofu on sweet potato puree with sauteed
boy choy and hoisin-ginger sauce, pg 65

stuffed poblano makhani

serves 6

Roasted poblano peppers filled with potato, cheese, raisins and spices, then baked with a fragrant tomato and cashew gravy.

Poblanos:

1½ pounds (675 g) yellow potatoes, peeled and quartered

1 tablespoon grapeseed oil

2 tablespoon unsalted butter

½ cup onion, chopped finely

2 cloves garlic, minced

⅓ cup roasted cashews

8 ounces (225 g) queso fresco or paneer, grated

¼ cup cilantro (coriander leaves), chopped finely

1 teaspoon garam masala

2 teaspoons coriander seed, ground

1 teaspoon chili powder

1/3 cup raisins (sultanas)

1½ teaspoons salt

12 poblano peppers*

Place the poblanos under a broiler (grill) until blistered and well charred. Place the peppers in a sealed container for a minimum of 15 minutes, to steam for easier skin removal. Using a knife, carefully remove the entire stem (including the base) and gently remove the seeds from inside the peppers. Then carefully remove the outer papery skin of peppers.

Meanwhile, boil the potatoes until easily pierced with a fork and drain for 5 minutes or more. Mash the potatoes in a large bowl and set aside. Heat the butter and sauté the onions until golden. Add the garlic, raisins and cashews and sauté for a few minutes longer. Add to the potatoes along with the cheese, cilantro, spices and salt, and mix thoroughly.

makhani gravy:

4 tablespoon grapeseed oil

1 cup onion, chopped

28-ounce (800 g) can peeled tomatoes

½ tablespoon garlic, chopped

1 tablespoon ginger, chopped

¼ teaspoon cayenne pepper

1 tablespoon coriander seed, ground

2 teaspoons ground cumin

1 teaspoon ground cardamom

¼ teaspoon ground cinnamon

¼ teaspoon freshly ground black pepper

2 tablespoons unsalted butter

2 teaspoons white sugar

1 teaspoon salt, or to taste

½ teaspoon garam masala

⅓ cup + 2 tablespoons cream, divided

¼ cup chopped cilantro (coriander leaves) for garnish

In a medium heavy-bottomed saucepan, heat the oil and sauté the onion, garlic, ginger and salt over medium-low heat until golden brown.

continued on next page

Add the cayenne pepper, turmeric, coriander seed, cumin, cardamom, cinnamon, garam masala and pepper and cook for 1 minute, stirring constantly so the spices don't burn.

Crush the tomatoes by hand and add along with 1½ cups of water and the butter. Bring to a boil, then simmer for approximately 30 minutes, stirring often until reduced and thickened.

Remove from the heat and allow to cool. Blend until very smooth, then use the bottom of a ladle to push the sauce through a fine-meshed sieve into a saucepan. Add the sugar and cream and keep warm.

to finish: Heat oven to 350°F (175°C). In an oven-proof dish, pour enough makhani gravy to just cover the bottom of the dish. Fill the peppers with the potato stuffing and lay in a single layer in the baking dish. If some of the peppers are broken, just patch them together as best you can. Cover the poblanos evenly with the remaining gravy. Cover the dish with aluminum foil and bake for 20 minutes. Remove from the oven, garnish with chopped cilantro and serve.

If you are unable to find poblano peppers you may substitute with green sweet Italian peppers or small green bell peppers. Roast peppers in a 375°F (190°C) oven until blackened in spots and tender. Then follow instructions above for skin removal.

roasted vegetable and cheese strudel with tomato coulis

serves 10-12

9 tablespoons olive oil, divided

2 medium zucchini

1 large eggplant, peeled and cut into ½-inch (1.25 cm) dice

2 red bell peppers (capsicums), cut into ½-inch (1.25 cm) dice

2½ cups onion, cut into ½-inch (1.25 cm) dice

1 pound (450 g) cremini (Swiss brown) mushrooms cut into ½-inch (1.25 cm) dice

1½ tablespoons garlic, chopped finely

1 cup roughly chopped basil leaves

8 ounces (225 g) goat cheese, at room temperature

8 ounces (225 g) firm ricotta cheese

½ cup Parmigiano-Reggiano cheese, grated

3 eggs, lightly beaten

1 cup panko bread crumbs

½ teaspoon freshly ground black pepper

1 teaspoon salt or to taste

1 packet phyllo pastry*

2 ounces (60 g) unsalted butter

Heat the oven to 375°F (190°C). Place the zucchini, eggplant, bell peppers and onion in a bowl and toss with 4 tablespoons of oil. Season with salt and pepper. Spread between two parchment-lined baking trays so vegetables are in a single layer. Place the trays in the oven and bake until golden and eggplant is tender, about 45 minutes. Switch the tray positions from upper and lower racks half way though cooking time. Remove from the oven and cool.

Meanwhile, heat 2 tablespoons of oil in a sauté pan and sauté the garlic over medium-low heat for a few minutes then add the mushrooms and sauté over a medium-high heat until soft, golden brown and all the liquid has evaporated. Place in a large bowl along with the roasted vegetables and leave to cool. In a separate bowl, mix together the basil, goat cheese, ricotta cheese, Parmigiano-Reggiano, eggs, bread crumbs, salt and pepper. Add vegetables, mix well and refrigerate for 30 minutes.

Melt the butter with 3 tablespoons of olive oil. Lay a single sheet of phyllo pastry on a work surface with the longest side facing you and brush the entire surface with the butter and oil mix. Lay a second sheet on top of the first and brush with butter and oil. Repeat until you have 5 sheets layered and brushed with butter and oil. Lay half the filling in a log shape across the center of the pastry, leaving 2 inches (5 cm) at either end.

Fold the phyllo edge closest to you over the filling. Brush the surface with butter and oil. Fold in both of the short ends and gently roll forward to completely encase the filling into a tight roll. Place on a parchment-lined baking tray and repeat the process again so you have two strudel rolls on the tray. Brush the entire surface of both strudels with butter and oil and bake for 40-50 minutes until golden brown.

continued on next page

Let cool for 15 minutes before cutting. Cut 1 inch (2.5 cm) from each of the short ends and discard. Cut each strudel into portions and serve with roasted tomato coulis.

tomato coulis

4 pounds (1.8 kg) ripe Roma (plum) tomatoes, cored and halved lengthwise

4 tablespoons olive oil

1½ tablespoons fresh thyme, chopped

6 cloves garlic, peeled and thinly sliced

2 teaspoons kosher salt

freshly ground black pepper

½ teaspoon sugar

4 tablespoons cold unsalted butter

Heat the oven to 375°F (190°C).
Line a baking tray with parchment paper. Place the tomatoes in a bowl with the oil, thyme, garlic, salt and pepper, then place on the tray in a single layer, cut side down. Roast the tomatoes for approximately 45 minutes, or until soft and beginning to brown. Remove from the oven and cool.

Push the tomatoes through a food mill and discard the seeds and skins. Alternately, process the tomatoes in a food processor until smooth and pour into a sieve. Using the bottom of a soup ladle, push the tomato pulp through the sieve. Place the purée in a saucepan and simmer for 15 minutes. Add the butter 1 tablespoon at a time until melted. Adjust the seasoning with salt and pepper and add sugar. Ladle ⅓ cup per person onto a plate, then place a serving of strudel on top.

Look for phyllo pastry sheets that are about 15 inches (37.5 cm) long. These large sheets may be a little wide, so to avoid too much pastry wrapping around the filling, trim off an inch (2.5 cm) or so on the longside of the pastry. The pastry should overlap by about 2 inches (5 cm) to encase filling properly; the remainder is excess.

potato roesti with sautéed mushrooms, poached eggs and sauce meurette

Eggs are not just for breakfast! Though this would be a pretty sensational brunch offering. Eggs are the perfect meal for vegetarians and a nice change from beans or tofu as a protein source. This recipe looks complex at first glance, though everything can be made ahead or the day before. Sauce meurette is a classic French red wine sauce most often served with poached eggs. It tastes wonderful combined with a crispy potato pancake, sautéed mushrooms and a crisp green salad.

serves 6

sauce meurette:

1 bottle, fruity red wine

2 cups water

1 onion

2 carrots

1 celery stick

2 garlic cloves

1 bay leaf

1 sprig parsley

1 sprig rosemary

1 sprig thyme

6 peppercorns

1 tablespoon tomato paste

3 tablespoons unsalted butter

3 tablespoons all-purpose (plain) flour

1 teaspoon balsamic vinegar

salt and pepper to taste

roesti:

2 pounds (900 g) russet potatoes, peeled

1 small onion, grated

1 tablespoon fresh thyme, grated

ghee or olive oil

1 teaspoon salt

¼ teaspoon freshly ground pepper

mushrooms:

2 tablespoons olive oil

3 pounds (1.45 kg) assorted mushrooms (shiitake, cremini/Swiss brown, chanterelle etc)

2 tablespoons unsalted butter

1 cup (French) shallots, chopped finely

3 cloves garlic, chopped finely

2 teaspoons thyme, chopped finely

eggs:

12 fresh free range eggs

sauce: Combine the first 11 ingredients into a large pot and bring to a boil. Reduce heat to medium and simmer for approximately 40 minutes or until liquid has reduced by half. Strain well by pressing the vegetables to extract as much liquid and flavor as possible. Discard the vegetables. In a saucepan, melt the butter, add the flour and cook gently until lightly golden. Add the wine mixture and tomato paste and whisk well. Bring to a boil and cook, stirring often, until thickened. Add the salt and pepper and balsamic vinegar.

roesti: Parboil the potatoes in salted water until just tender, but not soft. Allow to cool and chill in the fridge for at least a couple of hours or overnight. *Continued on next page*

Coarsely grate the potatoes, add the onion and thyme, and season with salt and pepper. Heat enough ghee in a large non-stick frying pan to just cover the surface. Divide the potato mix into 6 handfuls, then shape into shallow cakes about ¾ inch (1.8 cm thick. Add as many handfuls as can fit comfortably into the frying pan and fry without moving for about 5 minutes so they form a golden crust. Flip over and continue to cook for 7 minutes more, turning once or twice more if you need to until they are golden and crisp. You may need to add more ghee if the pan becomes dry. Roesti can be made ahead, then re-heated in the oven.

mushrooms: Wash the mushrooms and remove the stems. Quarter or halve the mushrooms. Heat 2 tablespoons of oil in a large sauté pan over medium-high heat and sauté the mushrooms in batches, being careful not to overcrowd the pan. Sauté until golden brown, remove and set aside. Repeat with the

pan-fried ricotta polenta with ratatouille

Ratatouille is such a great accompaniment to so many dishes. It is full of color, flavor and deliciously juicy. Served with pan-fried polenta filled with creamy ricotta and Parmigiano - Reggiano. Add a side of sautéed broccoli rabe and you have a great meal.

serves 6

3 tablespoons olive oil

2 medium onions

1 green bell pepper (capsicum)

1 red bell pepper (capsicum)

4 cloves garlic, minced

1 medium eggplant

2 medium zucchini

1 fennel bulb

2 pounds (900 g) ripe tomatoes, peeled and chopped (about 4 large)

1½ teaspoons salt, or to taste

¼ teaspoon freshly ground black pepper

½ cup white wine

12 green or black pitted olives

1 teaspoon white sugar

½ cup fresh basil, sliced finely

3 tablespoons parsley, chopped

Dice the onion, bell peppers, zucchini, fennel, tomato and eggplant into ¾ inch (1.8 cm) cubes. In a large saucepan, heat 2 tablespoons of oil and sauté the onion, bell pepper and garlic over medium heat until golden brown. Remove from the pan and set aside. Add 2 more tablespoons of oil and sauté the zucchini and fennel until golden brown. Repeat with the eggplant. In a large, deep sauté pan, add the tomatoes, sautéed vegetables, sugar, basil, wine, olives, salt and pepper and bring to a boil. Reduce heat and simmer for 30-40 minutes, stirring often until the vegetables are tender, then remove from heat.

polenta:

1½ cups coarse polenta*

5 cups water

2 cups ricotta cheese

½ cup grated Parmigiano-Reggiano cheese

2 teaspoons salt, or to taste

continued on next page

Pour the water into a heavy-bottomed pot, bring to a boil and add salt. Gradually pour the polenta into the saucepan while whisking to ensure no lumps form. Return to a boil, then reduce to a low simmer, stirring frequently with a wooden spoon, for about 20-25 minutes.

Add the ricotta and Parmigiano-Reggiano cheeses and mix well. Rinse a 12" x 8" (30 x 20 cm) sheet pan and shake off the water. Spread the polenta evenly onto tray and leave to cool for 1 hour.

When ready to serve cut polenta into 4"x 4" (10 cm x 10 cm) squares. Heat a large non-stick pan and add oil until it just covers the bottom of the pan. Cook the polenta over medium-high heat until brown and crispy, then flip and cook the other side. This should take at least 5 minutes, which will ensure the center is nice and hot. Remove from the pan and keep warm. Add additional oil to the frying pan and repeat. Place 2 squares of polenta on each plate and top with ratatouille and grated Parmigiano-Reggiano cheese.

The addition of ricotta only works with coarse polenta. Any other variation of polenta will be too soft to pan-fry.

N.B. If you refrigerate the polenta overnight, bring it up to room temperature and pat it dry before pan-frying.

pan-fried ricotta polenta with ratatouille, pg 73

lentil and mushroom croquettes with red bell pepper gastrique

makes 10 (serves 3-5)

croquettes:

1 cup red lentils, rinsed and drained

2 tablespoons olive oil, plus extra for frying

1 large onion, chopped finely (1½ cups)

6 cloves garlic, chopped finely

1 pound (450 g) cremini (Swiss brown) or portobello mushrooms

1 teaspoon salt

1 teaspoon dried marjoram

1 teaspoon dried basil

2 tablespoons lemon juice

½ cup parsley, chopped finely

2 eggs, lightly beaten

½ cup grated Parmigiano-Reggiano cheese

1 cup panko bread crumbs

Put the lentils and 3 cups water into a small saucepan. Bring to a boil, then simmer uncovered for 15 minutes, stirring occasionally. Pour the lentils into a sieve and drain for at least 30 minutes.

Heat 2 tablespoons of oil in a large frying pan and sauté the onions over medium-low heat until golden brown. Add the garlic and cook for two minutes, then add the mushrooms, salt, marjoram and basil and continue to cook until the mushrooms begin to brown slightly and all the liquid has evaporated. Mix in the parsley, remove from the frying pan and cool.

In a large bowl mix the lentils, mushrooms, eggs, lemon juice, Parmigiano-Reggiano cheese and bread crumbs. Refrigerate for 1 hour. Take a small handful (about ½ cup) and form an oval shaped patty about ½ inch (1.25 cm) thick. Repeat until all the mixture is used.

Pour 2 tablespoons of oil into a non-stick frying pan over medium heat and cook both sides of the croquette until nicely browned, about 2-3 minutes per side. Repeat with the remaining croquettes, adding extra oil to pan as needed.

Serve the croquettes with warm bell pepper gastrique.

red bell pepper gastrique

makes about 2 cups

2 tablespoons oil

2 medium (French) shallots, chopped finely

2 garlic cloves, sliced

1 tablespoon white sugar

2 red bell peppers (capsicums)

1¼ cups vegetable stock or water

⅓ cup red wine vinegar

½ teaspoon salt, or to taste

¼ teaspoon black pepper, ground

2 tablespoons cold unsalted butter

Heat the oven to 375°F (175°C). Place the bell peppers on an aluminum foil-lined tray and roast for 40 minutes. Remove and place in a sealed plastic bag or a heat-proof container and allow the peppers to steam for 10 minutes. Allow to cool, remove the skins and seeds, and chop roughly. Don't be tempted to wash the peppers under water to remove the seeds, as this also removes a lot of flavor that developed while roasting. *Continued on next page*

76

Heat the oil in a small saucepan and gently sauté the shallots and garlic until golden brown. Add the sugar and cook until it begins to caramelize. Slowly add the vinegar and cook until the vinegar has almost evaporated. Add the bell peppers and stock. Bring to a boil and simmer for 10 minutes.

mushroom stroganov with teff spaetzle and sautéed tuscan kale

serves 4

stroganov and kale:

2 tablespoons olive oil

1 tablespoon unsalted butter

2 pounds (900 g) assorted mushrooms: cremini/Swiss brown, shiitake, etc.

½ cup (French) shallots, chopped finely

¼ cup dry sherry

1 teaspoon fresh thyme, chopped finely

1 tablespoons tomato paste

2 teaspoons Worcestershire sauce

2 teaspoons Dijon mustard

1 teaspoon paprika

1½ cups vegetable stock

1 tablespoon all-purpose (plain) flour

¼ cup sour cream

salt and pepper to taste

1 bunch lacinato (Tuscan) kale

Wash the mushrooms and remove the stems. Cut into ¼-inch (0.6 cm) slices and set aside. Heat 1 tablespoon oil in a large frying pan and add half the mushrooms. Sauté over high heat until they are golden and any liquid from mushrooms has evaporated. Remove from the pan and repeat with the remaining mushrooms.

Reduce the heat to medium and add the butter, then sauté the onions until they are translucent. Add the garlic and thyme and sauté for 1 minute. Return the mushrooms to pan and add the sherry. Cook over high heat until all the liquid has evaporated. In a bowl, whisk together the tomato paste, paprika, mustard, Worcestershire sauce, flour and vegetable stock. Bring to a boil, then reduce the heat and simmer for 10 minutes. Add the sour cream and season with salt and pepper. Remove from the heat and set aside.

Wash the kale and strip the leaves from the stems. Roughly tear the kale into approximately 2-3 inch (5-7.5 cm) pieces. In a sauté pan, heat 1 tablespoon olive oil and season the oil with ½ teaspoon salt and a few grinds of black pepper. Add the kale and sauté along with any water remaining on leaves. Cover, reduce the heat to very low and steam until tender, adding water as needed.

teff spaetzle:

¾ cup teff flour (see sources)

2 ¼ cups all-purpose (plain) flour

½ cup ricotta cheese

6 eggs

1 cup water

1½ teaspoons kosher salt

½ teaspoon freshly ground black pepper

continued on next page

77

2-3 tablespoons unsalted butter

In a large bowl, combine both flours, and the salt and pepper. In another mixing bowl, whisk the eggs and water together. Make a well in the center of the dry ingredients and pour in the egg-water mixture. Gradually draw in the flour from the sides and combine well; the dough should be smooth and thick. Cover with plastic wrap and let the dough rest in the refrigerator for 1 hour or overnight.

Bring 3 quarts of salted water to a boil in a large pot, then reduce to a simmer. To form the spaetzle, hold a large-holed colander over the simmering water and push the dough through the holes with a spatula or spoon. Do this in batches so you don't overcrowd the pot. Cook for 3 to 4 minutes or until the spaetzle float to the surface, stirring gently to prevent sticking. Dump the spaetzle into a colander and give them a quick rinse with cold water and drain well.

Melt the butter in a large frying pan over medium heat and add the spaetzle, tossing to coat. Cook the spaetzle for 1 to 2 minutes over high heat to give the noodles some color. Season with additional salt and pepper to taste.

assembly: Mix the kale with the finished spaetzle. Mound on individual plates, then top with stroganoff and serve.

on the side

balsamic glazed carrots

I could eat fresh organic broccoli or green beans any day with just a little olive oil, salt and freshly ground black pepper, but not carrots. In my opinion cooked carrots are nice only in small amounts, unless you give them the royal treatment of balsamic, butter and maple syrup.

serves 4-6

1 tablespoons olive oil

2 tablespoons unsalted butter

2 pounds (900 g) baby or Dutch carrots, tops removed, peeled*

3 cloves garlic, sliced finely

2 teaspoons fresh thyme, chopped

3 tablespoons maple syrup

3 tablespoons balsamic vinegar

½ teaspoon salt, or to taste

freshly ground black pepper

Cut the carrots into ½-inch (1.25 cm) slices on the diagonal. Heat the oil in a large sauté pan over medium-high heat and sauté the carrots, stirring often until golden brown in places. Remove the carrots from the pan and set aside. In the same pan, add the butter, thyme, garlic, maple syrup, balsamic vinegar, salt and pepper. Return the carrots to the pan and toss well to coat. Add salt and pepper to taste, and continue to cook over medium-low heat, stirring often until the carrots are tender, the liquid has evaporated and a thick glaze coats the carrots.

*In the U.S., Dutch carrots are small carrots that are sold in bunches with the leaves intact.

braised favas, fennel and artichokes

This dish is all about spring, full of flavor and texture! Serve with plenty of crusty bread to mop up the juices.

serves 4 (vegan)

4 tablespoons extra virgin olive oil

1 large red onion, cut into 8 wedges

2 cloves garlic, finely chopped

2 tablespoons chopped parsley

8 baby artichokes, trimmed and quartered (see basic ingredients and techniques)

2 lemons

1 large fennel bulb, halved lengthwise, core removed, and sliced thickly crosswise

1 pound (450 g) fava beans, shelled but not peeled

½ pound (225 g) fresh peas, shelled

¼ pound (110 g) shredded greens, such as curly endive, spinach or chicory

salt and freshly ground black pepper

fresh Parmigiano-Reggiano, grated, to serve

continued on next page

80

Combine the oil and onion in a large casserole dish and cook over moderate heat until soft, about 8 minutes. Add the garlic and parsley and cook further 1 minute. Stir in the artichokes and cook a few minutes, and repeat with the fennel. Stir in the fava beans and peas, then the greens, and stir until the greens start to wilt. Add enough water to cover the vegetables and season with salt and pepper. Bring to a boil, then simmer with the lid ajar until the vegetables are tender, about 20-30 minutes, stirring occasionally. Adjust the seasoning and serve drizzled with extra virgin olive oil and sprinkled with Parmigiano-Reggiano cheese.

sweet corn fritters

These are great as a side dish, or make mini fritters and top with guacamole for an appetizer. It also makes for a delicious breakfast idea (see page 3)

makes approximately 12

¼ cup grapeseed oil

3 ears sweet corn

3 tablespoons cilantro (coriander leaves), chopped

1-2 Jalapeño chili, chopped finely

3 scallions, (spring onions), sliced finely

2 large eggs, lightly beaten

⅓ cup milk

1 cup sharp cheddar cheese, grated

½ teaspoon salt

½ cup all-purpose (plain) flour

1 teaspoon baking powder

Bring water to a boil in a medium sized pot. Cook the corn for 3-5 minutes or until tender. Remove from the pot and allow to cool before cutting off the kernels.

In a medium sized bowl, mix together all the wet ingredients. In a separate bowl, mix together the flour, salt and baking powder. Fold the flour into wet ingredients. The mixture should be fairly thick.

In a medium to large non-stick frying pan add enough oil to cover the bottom of the frying pan and heat on a medium heat. Add heaped tablespoons of corn batter and flatten into ½-inch (1.25 cm) discs. Cook each side for approximately 2-3 minutes or until deep golden brown, then place on paper towels.

green beans braised in tomato with cinnamon and allspice

I fell in love with these beans over 30 years ago. Every Lebanese restaurant in Sydney has their own version. The green beans are braised until they just melt in your mouth. Serve cold or at room temperature.

serves 4 (vegan)

¼ cup extra virgin olive oil

1½ pounds (675 g) green beans

3 cups ripe tomatoes, skins removed and chopped

1 medium onion, chopped finely

4 cloves garlic, chopped finely

1 tablespoon white sugar

1 teaspoon salt

½ cup water

1½ teaspoons cinnamon, ground

¾ teaspoon allspice, ground

In a large frying pan over medium-low heat, add the oil and sauté the onions until translucent. Add the garlic, cinnamon and allspice and sauté gently for 1 minute. Add the tomatoes and their juice, sugar, salt and water and mix well. Add the green beans, mix well and bring to a boil. Cover and reduce heat to a simmer. Simmer gently for 45 minutes stirring occasionally until the beans are very tender. Remove the lid after 30 minutes to reduce liquid.

roasted potatoes pimentón

serves 4 (vegan)

2½ pounds (1.1 kg) yellow potatoes, such as Yukon Gold, skin on

¼ cup olive oil

2 teaspoon pimentón (sweet smoked paprika)

1 teaspoon garlic powder

2 teaspoon chili powder

1 teaspoon cumin powder

1½ teaspoons salt

2 tablespoons red wine vinegar

Heat oven to 400°F (200°C).

Mix together the pimentón, garlic, chili, cumin and salt and set aside.

Line a rimmed sheet tray with parchment paper.

Cut the potatoes into wedges (approximately ¾ inch (1.8 cm) wide) depending on the size. Try to keep the potato wedges relatively the same size. Place the potatoes in a large bowl. Add the olive oil to potatoes and mix well. Sprinkle the spice mix over the potatoes and mix well with your hands.

Spread the potatoes evenly in a single layer on the prepared tray. Bake until golden brown and tender, approximately 50 minutes. Sprinkle the potatoes evenly with vinegar and toss gently.

sautéed kale with shiitake mushrooms

Dark leafy greens are so good for you that it is worth trying different ways to keep them interesting. Even though the ingredients are distinctly Asian, the flavors are subtle and will compliment most menus.

serves 4 (vegan)

2 large bunches curly kale, ribs removed and chopped roughly

1½ tablespoons grapeseed oil

½ pound (225 g) fresh shiitake mushrooms

4 cloves garlic, peeled and chopped finely

½ teaspoon dried chili flakes

2 tablespoons soy sauce

1 tablespoon maple syrup

½ teaspoon salt

2 teaspoons toasted sesame oil

Bring a large pot of salted water to a boil. Cook the kale until tender and drain.

Meanwhile remove the stems from the shiitakes and cut into ½-inch (1.25 cm) slices. Heat the oil in a large non-stick sauté pan and sauté mushrooms and garlic over medium-high heat until the mushrooms begin to change color. Add the remaining ingredients and mix well. Add the kale and sauté together for a few minutes for flavors to meld before serving.

sautéed spinach with black mission figs

I tasted this dish at a tapas bar and thought the sweet figs, earthy spinach, and splash of vinegar was a delicious combo.

serves 4 (vegan)

2 pounds (900 g) spinach, washed and thick stems removed

5 cloves garlic, sliced thinly

8 dried black mission figs

4 tablespoons olive oil

2 tablespoons honey

1 tablespoon sherry vinegar

½ teaspoon freshly ground black pepper

1 teaspoon kosher salt

Soak the figs in room temperature water for 1 hour. Drain and discard the water. Remove the hard nub at the end of the stem and cut the figs in half, then set aside.

In a large wide pot, heat the oil and gently sauté the garlic until light golden in color. Add the spinach and salt, increase the heat to medium-high, and sauté until wilted and tender.

With a slotted spoon, remove the spinach and set aside, leaving the water behind in the pot. Add the figs, pepper, honey and vinegar to the pot and increase the heat, stirring frequently until the liquid has mostly evaporated and thickened. Return the spinach to pot and gently mix.

quinoa pilaf

Commonly, cooking instructions for quinoa suggest a 1:2 ratio of grain to water which always gives a soggy result. Here is a great way to prepare quinoa that is flavourful, light and fluffy.

serves 4-6 (vegan)

2-3 tablespoons unsalted butter or olive oil

1 cup finely diced onion

1 medium carrot, peeled and cut into small dice

1 celery stick, cut into small dice

2 cloves garlic, chopped finely

2 teaspoons fresh thyme, chopped finely

1 bay leaf

2½ cups vegetable stock

1½ cups quinoa, rinsed and drained

1 teaspoon salt, or to taste

few grinds of pepper

1 cup parsley, chopped finely

Heat the oil in a medium saucepan and sauté the onion, carrot and celery until the onions are translucent. Add the garlic and thyme, sauté for a minute, then add the stock, bay leaf, salt and pepper. Bring to a boil and add the quinoa. When it comes to a boil again, cover and reduce to a slow simmer. Cook for 18 minutes, then leave the lid on for another 10 minutes before folding in the parsley.

quinoa with roasted cauliflower and olives

serves 6 (vegan)

2 small heads cauliflower

¼ cup + 3 tablespoons olive oil

1 cup finely diced onion

2 cloves garlic, chopped finely

2½ cups vegetable stock

1 bay leaf

1 large strip lemon peel

2 teaspoons fresh thyme, chopped finely

1½ cups quinoa, rinsed and drained

1 teaspoon salt, or to taste

few grinds of pepper

1 cup parsley, chopped finely

1 cup pitted green olives, halved

Heat the oven to 400°F (200°C). Cut the cauliflower into small florets, toss with ¼ cup olive oil, and season with salt and pepper. Place the cauliflower in a single layer on a parchment- or aluminum-lined baking tray and roast until tender and golden brown, about 40 minutes. Keep warm.

In a medium saucepan, heat 3 tablespoons olive oil and sauté the onion until golden. Add the garlic and sauté for 2 minutes. Add the stock, bay leaf, lemon peel, salt and pepper, and bring to a boil. Add the quinoa, and when it comes to a boil again, reduce to a slow simmer. Cook for 18 minutes, then leave the lid on for 5-10 minutes before folding in the cauliflower, olives and parsley.

quinoa vegetable biryani

serves 6 (vegan)

3 tablespoons grapeseed oil

3 whole cloves

4 whole green cardamom pods, lightly crushed

1 cinnamon stick

1 bay leaf

1 medium onion, sliced finely

1 teaspoon garlic, minced

2 teaspoons fresh ginger, minced

1 jalapeño chili, minced

½ teaspoon ground cumin

2 teaspoons ground coriander seed

¼ teaspoon turmeric

½ teaspoon garam masala

½ teaspoon chili powder (optional)

1 ½ teaspoons salt

½ cup frozen green peas

1 cup cauliflower, cut into small florets

½ cup carrots cut into ¼-inch (0.6 cm) dice

2½ cups water

2 tablespoon lemon juice

2 tablespoons raisins (sultanas)

3 tablespoons roasted cashews, split in half

1½ cups quinoa, rinsed and drained

¼ cup fresh cilantro (coriander leaves), chopped

Heat the oil in a wide saucepan or deep sauté pan over medium heat. Add the cloves, cardamom and cinnamon. Sauté for 10 seconds, then add onion. Sauté the onion until it becomes light golden brown.

Add the garlic, ginger and chili and cook for 1 minute. Add the cumin, coriander seed, turmeric, garam masala, chili powder, salt and all the vegetables. Sauté for 2 minutes. Add the water, lemon juice, raisins, cashews and quinoa. Bring to a boil, then cover. Reduce heat to very low and cook for 20 minutes. Remove from heat and keep covered for an additional 10 minutes. Fluff with a fork and garnish with chopped cilantro.

rice pilaf with carrots, currants, pine nuts and dill

A classic Turkish pilaf. Try it with braised green beans and tomato (see page 82) served with a dollop of yoghurt.

serves 6 (vegan*)

2 tablespoons olive oil

⅓ cup pine nuts, toasted

2 tablespoons unsalted butter

1 cup onion, chopped finely

1-2 medium carrots, peeled and sliced ¼ inch (0.6 cm) thick, approximately 1 cup

2 cloves garlic, chopped finely

⅓ cup currants

1½ cups basmati rice

2½ cups water

1 teaspoon ground cinnamon

1½ teaspoons salt

1½ teaspoons white sugar

freshly ground black pepper

¼ cup fresh dill or parsley, chopped

Wash the rice well in several changes of water. Cover with water and soak for 20 minutes. Drain well.

Heat the olive oil in a frying pan and sauté the pine nuts over medium heat until golden brown. Remove from the frying pan and set aside.

In a medium saucepan with a tight fitting lid heat the butter, then sauté the onion, carrots and garlic until the onions are translucent. Add the currants, salt, pepper, sugar and rice and sauté for a few minutes. Add the water, bring to a boil, then cover and reduce to a very low heat. Simmer for 18 minutes. Turn off heat and do not remove lid for another 10 minutes. Fluff with a fork, mix in the dill or parsley, and cover again for 5 minutes. Spoon the rice onto a platter, then sprinkle with pine nuts.

*vegan: substitute butter with olive oil

roasted potatoes pimenton pg 82

braised carrots with tomato and thyme

Carrots slow cooked in the oven with wine tomato and herbs until they melt in your mouth.

serves 4 (vegan)

3 tablespoons olive oil, divided

1 pound (450 g) medium-sized carrots, peeled, halved lengthwise, cut into 2-inch (5 cm) lengths

3 celery sticks, cut into 2-inch (5 cm) lengths

1 medium Spanish or red onion, sliced thinly

2 cloves garlic, peeled and sliced

1 cup peeled tomatoes, crushed by hand

½ cup white wine

2 teaspoons fresh thyme, chopped

1 bay leaf

1 teaspoon salt

freshly ground black pepper

Heat oven to 350°F (175°C). Heat 3 tablespoons of oil in a large oven-proof sauté pan over medium-high heat. Sauté the onions, celery and garlic, stirring often, until golden brown. Remove from the pan. Add the remaining oil and sauté the carrots until they begin to turn golden brown in places. Return the sautéed onions and celery to the pan and add the tomatoes, wine, thyme, bay leaves, salt and pepper. Bring to a boil, cover, and braise in the oven for approximately 50 minutes or until very tender. Alternatively, bring to a boil, empty the contents into a casserole dish, cover and bake according to the directions above.

fennel braised in orange juice

serves 6-8 (vegan*)

4 large fennel bulbs, about 1½ pounds (675 g)

1 tablespoon olive oil

1 tablespoon unsalted butter

½ teaspoon curry powder

1 cup vegetable stock

½ cup fresh orange juice (about 1 orange)

1 teaspoon sherry vinegar

½ teaspoon salt

⅛ teaspoon freshly ground black pepper

2 tablespoons chopped fennel fronds

Peel the outside of the fennel bulbs and trim off the root from bottom, leaving enough so the wedges hold together. Trim the stalks from the top, reserving the fennel fronds for garnish. Cut each bulb into 8 wedges.

Heat the oil and butter in a large frying pan over medium heat and cook the fennel in a single layer until golden on both sides.
Sprinkle with the curry powder, salt and pepper, flip over fennel and cook on low heat for one minute.

Add the vegetable stock, orange juice and vinegar. Reduce the heat, and simmer covered for 20 minutes or until tender, turning fennel after the first 10 minutes. Remove the lid and continue to cook until the liquid almost evaporates and fennel is very tender. Sprinkle with the fennel fronds and serve.

vegan: substitute butter with olive oil

sautéed sweet corn, zucchini and bell peppers with cilantro and lime

serves 4

4 tablespoons olive oil, divided

3 ears fresh sweet corn, cooked and kernels removed

2 red bell peppers (capsicums), cut into ¼-inch (0.6 cm) dice

2 medium zucchini, cut into ¼-inch (0.6 cm) dice

1 large red onion, cut into ¼-inch (0.6 cm) dice

1 large clove garlic, chopped finely

2 teaspoons ancho chili powder (see sources)

½ teaspoon cumin powder

juice of half a lime

salt to taste

⅓ cup cilantro (coriander leaves), chopped

Heat 2 tablespoons oil in a large frying pan over medium heat and add the onions and bell peppers. Sauté, stirring often, until light golden brown and softened. Remove and set aside. Heat 2 tablespoons of oil in the same pan and cook the zucchini until golden brown. Add the garlic, chili and cumin, and continue stirring for about 1 minute. Add the corn, onions and bell peppers, and mix well. Remove from the heat and add lime juice, cilantro and salt to taste.

roasted cauliflower florets with porcini mushroom and cheese crust

serves 4

2 small or 1 large cauliflower

3 cloves garlic, minced

4 tablespoons olive oil

½ ounce (15 g) dried porcini mushrooms

⅔ cup Parmigiano-Reggiano cheese, finely grated

1 teaspoon salt

1 teaspoon white sugar

3 tablespoons chopped parsley

Preheat the oven to 400°F (200°C).

Cut the cauliflower into florets about 2 inches (5 cm) wide and place in a large bowl. In a small bowl, mix the garlic and olive oil, then mix with cauliflower and set aside. Grind porcini to a powder then mix 3 tablespoons of porcini powder with salt and sugar and sprinkle over cauliflower whilst mixing.

Spread out the cauliflower in a single layer on 2 parchment-lined baking trays. Leave a good amount of space between the florets so they don't steam. Roast in the oven for 15 minutes, then flip the cauliflower and swap the positions of the trays around: place the bottom tray on top rack and vice versa. Roast for a further 15 minutes or until tender. Remove from the oven, sprinkle with parmesan and return to oven for 5 minutes. Remove from oven, sprinkle with parsley and serve.

maple roasted parsnips

I've never been a huge fan of parsnips. I think it's because my mum never cooked them when I was growing up. Roasted with maple syrup, though, they're pretty awesome.

2 pounds (900 g) parsnips, peeled

2 tablespoons grapeseed oil

4 tablespoons maple syrup

1 teaspoon salt

freshly ground black pepper

Heat the oven to 400°F (200°C).
Cut the parsnips in half crossways, then cut the larger top end into quarters. The parsnip pieces should all be relatively the same size. Toss with oil, then salt and pepper. Drizzle over the maple syrup and toss again. Place on a parchment lined baking tray and bake for 20 minutes, then toss them around a bit. Continue to cook for another 20 minutes until deep golden brown and tender. Adjust the seasoning if needed and serve.

ratatouille masala

Spices can add another dimension of flavor to classic dishes. Here is a famous French provincial dish that marries very well with Indian spices.

serves 5-6 (vegan)

6 tablespoons olive oil

1 medium onion

1 yellow bell pepper (capsicum)

1 red bell pepper (capsicum)

1 medium eggplant

2 medium zucchini

4 cloves garlic, minced

1 14-ounce (400 g) can diced tomatoes

1½-2 tablespoons Madras curry powder

1½ teaspoons salt

1 teaspoon red wine vinegar

2 teaspoons white sugar

4 tablespoons fresh basil, sliced finely (optional)

Chop the onion, bell peppers, zucchini and eggplant into ¾-inch (1.8 cm) cubes.
In a large saucepan, heat 2 tablespoons of the oil and sauté the onion, bell pepper and garlic on medium-high heat until softened; remove. Add 2 tablespoons oil and sauté the eggplant for 4-5 minutes until golden brown, then remove. Add 2 tablespoons oil and sauté the zucchini for 4-5 minutes or until golden brown. Add the curry powder and salt and sauté for a 1 minute. Return all the vegetables to the pan along with the tomatoes and bring to a boil.

Cover and reduce to a simmer. Simmer for 15-20 minutes or until the eggplant is very tender. Add the vinegar, sugar and basil, cook for a few minutes more and serve.

salads

baby spinach and roasted butternut squash salad with miso dressing

Equally good when you substitute baby kale for spinach. If you do use kale, leave the dressing on for at least 10 minutes so the kale has time to wilt and soften.

serves 4 (vegan)

4 cups butternut squash (pumpkin), cut into 1-inch (2.5 cm) cubes

1 tablespoon olive oil

3 ounces (90 g) baby spinach (4 big handfuls)

½ cup walnut halves

3 tablespoons white miso

3 tablespoons rice vinegar

2 teaspoons honey or agave

1 small clove garlic, minced

½ teaspoon toasted sesame oil

3 tablespoons water

2 tablespoons grapeseed oil

Preheat the oven 375°F (190°C). Toss the butternut squash with olive oil, then place on a baking tray and roast until tender and golden brown (approx 45-60 mins). Set aside to cool. Whisk together the miso, vinegar, honey, garlic, sesame oil, water and oil until smooth. Place the spinach, butternut and walnuts in a large bowl and drizzle over dressing to taste. Toss and serve immediately.

optional: throw in some walnuts for a nice crunch

roasted beet salad with beet greens, orzo pasta, feta and pine nuts

serves 6 (vegan*)

1½ cups orzo pasta

2 pounds (900 g) red beets with leaves attached

8 ounces (225 g) feta cheese

1 teaspoon olive oil

½ cup pine nuts

dressing:

¼ cup lemon juice

2 tablespoons white balsamic vinegar

¼ cup olive oil

1 tablespoon honey

½ teaspoon fine salt

¼ teaspoon black pepper, ground

1 clove garlic, chopped finely

Heat oven to 350°F (175°C). Remove the beet leaves from the beet root, then cut off and discard the stems. Wash the leaves well and set aside. Wash the beet roots, then wrap in aluminum foil so they are completely sealed.

Place on a oven tray and bake for an hour or more until they can be pierced easily with a fork. Unwrap the foil and cool. When cool, remove the skins, cut into ½ inch (1.25 cm) chunks and set aside.

Continued on next page

Bring a large pot of salted water to a boil and cook the beet leaves until just tender. Remove with tongs, rinse under cold water, then squeeze gently to remove most (but not all) of the water, then chop roughly. Return the water to a boil and cook the pasta according to the package directions. Drain, then rinse with cold water and let drain until ready to use.

Mix together the dressing ingredients. Place the pasta in a large bowl with the beets and leaves. Add dressing and mix well. Fold the feta cheese into the salad. Heat 1 teaspoon olive oil in a small frying pan and sauté the pine nuts over medium-low heat, stirring constantly, until golden brown. Fold into salad and serve.

vegan: omit feta cheese

butter lettuce with avocado, mango, cucumber, lime and sweet chili dressing

A refreshing salad on a hot day. I have used both ripe and semi-ripe mangoes and they both work well. As a tasty addition, you can also throw in some sharp cheddar.

serves 4 (vegan)

4 ounces (110 g) butter, boston or oak lettuce

½ small radicchio

2 small or 1 large ripe mango

1 ripe avocado, not too soft

½ seedless cucumber

½ small red onion

2 tablespoons Thai sweet chili sauce

2 tablespoons lime juice

2 tablespoons grapeseed oil

¼ teaspoon salt

Tear the lettuce and radicchio in half or quarters. Peel the mangoes and cut from the seed. With the cut side on the board, slice thinly crosswise and set aside. Cut the avocados into quarters and remove the skins and seeds. Slice thinly crosswise and set aside. Peel the cucumber, cut it in half lengthwise, and remove the seeds with a teaspoon. Cut thinly crosswise. Slice onion thinly. Whisk together the sweet chili sauce, lime juice and salt. Put all the above in a large bowl. Pour over the dressing to taste, toss lightly and serve immediately.

roasted beet salad with beet greens, orzo pasta, feta and pine nuts, pg 92

cold udon noodles with broccoli, tofu and pickled ginger

This makes a delicious one-dish meal on a summer day. It's perfectly balanced in nutrition and flavor. Don't feel limited to using only broccoli and carrot; it also works really well with asparagus and snow peas.

serves 4 (vegan)

dressing:

3 tablespoons soy sauce

3 tablespoons rice vinegar

1 tablespoon honey or agave nectar

1 tablespoon toasted sesame oil

2 cloves garlic, minced

2 tablespoons pickled ginger slices, julienned

1 tablespoon pickled ginger juice, drained from the pickles

noodles:

1 tablespoon sesame seeds

1 tablespoons, grapeseed oil

7 ounces (200 g) firm tofu, pressed *(see basic ingredients)*

2 tablespoons of soy sauce

3-4 cups broccoli, cut into small florets about 1 inch (2.5 cm) high

2 medium carrots

8 ounces (225 g) dried udon noodles or thin spaghetti.

⅓ cup scallions (spring onions), sliced thinly

Peel carrots, cut in half lengthwise then cut into ⅛ inch (0.3 cm) slices on the diagonal. Mix the dressing ingredients together and set aside.

Toast the sesame seeds in a frying pan, stirring constantly until golden. Remove from the frying pan and allow to cool.

Slice the tofu into ½-inch (1.25 cm) slices. In a non-stick frying pan add the oil. Heat over medium-high heat, then add the tofu and fry until golden on both sides. Splash with a few tablespoons of soy sauce and flip until well coated and the soy sauce has evaporated. Allow to cool, then cut into ½-inch (1.25 cm) cubes.

In a large pot of boiling water, cook the broccoli and carrots separately until crisp tender, place in iced water for a few minutes, then drain well. In the same pot, boil the udon noodles according to the package directions or until al dente. Drain and rinse under cold water, then drain well.

In a large bowl mix the noodles, vegetables, tofu and dressing together. Refrigerate until ready to eat, at least 30 minutes so it has time to marinate.

Toss again before serving and garnish with scallions and sesame seeds.

escarole, goat cheese, date salad with pomegranate dressing, pg 97

escarole, goat cheese, date and walnut salad with pomegranate dressing

Arugula can be substituted for escarole. Throw some radicchio in there as well for a splash of color and contrast to the sweet dates.

serves 4-6

1 head of escarole, cleaned (about 6 cups)

4 ounces (110 g) soft goat cheese

10 medjool dates, pitted and cut into 4

¾ cup walnuts

½ ripe pomegranate, seeded

dressing:

1 tablespoon pomegrante molasses

1 teaspoon red wine vinegar

3 tablespoon walnut oil or olive oil

1 tablespoon honey

2 tablespoons (French) shallots, chopped finely

½ teaspoon salt

Place walnuts on an ovenproof tray and bake at 350°F (175°C) for 10 minutes. Remove from oven and allow to cool.

Tear large leaves of escarole into halves or quarters. Place in a large bowl with the dates and walnuts. Whisk the dressing ingredients together and add enough dressing to taste. You may only need half.
Break the goat cheese into bite-sized chunks, scatter over the top of salad along with pomegranate seeds, and serve.

arugula salad with sautéed mushrooms, pear, celery, walnuts and shaved parmesan

A great fall salad I had at a local Italian restaurant; it has since become one of my favorites.

serves 4

4 packed cups wild arugula

2 sticks celery, sliced thinly

1 tablespoon olive oil

8 ounces (225 g) white mushrooms, washed, stem removed and sliced thinly

1 semi-ripe pear, cored and cut into matchsticks

⅓ cup walnuts

½ cup shaved Parmigiano-Reggiano

dressing:

2 tablespoons (French) shallot, chopped finely

1 teaspoon Dijon mustard

1 teaspoon honey

1 tablespoon white balsamic vinegar

3 tablespoons lemon juice

3 tablespoons olive oil

½ teaspoon salt

freshly ground black pepper to taste

In a large frying pan over a high heat, add 1 tablespoon of oil. Sauté the mushrooms briefly until they look golden brown in places. Remove from the pan and set aside.
Continued on next page

97

In a large bowl toss together the arugula, celery, mushrooms and pears. Whisk together the dressing ingredients and toss the salad in the dressing. Scatter the walnuts and shaved Parmigiano-Reggiano on top of the salad and serve.

kale salad with pine nuts, currants and shaved parmesan

A wonderful salad adapted from a recipe by Dan Barber of Blue Hill Farm.
Every time I make this salad no one can have enough of it. It really is addictive.

serves 6-8

2 tablespoons dried currants

2 tablespoons white balsamic vinegar, divided

1 tablespoon unseasoned rice vinegar

1 tablespoon honey

1½ tablespoons extra-virgin olive oil, divided

1 teaspoon salt

2 bunches lacinato (Tuscan) kale (about 1 pound or 450 g)

2 tablespoons pine nuts

½ cup or more Parmigiano-Reggiano cheese shavings

Place the currants, white balsamic vinegar and rice vinegar, in a small bowl and soak for several hours or overnight. Whisk in the honey, 1 tablespoon of oil, and the salt.

Heat ½ tablespoon olive oil in a small frying pan and sauté pine nuts over medium heat, stirring constantly, until they turn golden brown.

Remove the nuts from pan to stop them from cooking any further and set aside.

Remove center ribs and stems from kale and discard. Slice leaves crosswise in ½ inch (1.25 com) slices. Wash and spin dry. Place the kale and pine nuts in a large bowl, add all the dressing and toss to coat. Let marinate for 20 minutes at room temperature, tossing occasionally. Season to taste with salt and pepper. Sprinkle the cheese shavings over the salad and serve.

peanut sesame noodles

A classic asian salad. Noodles, crunchy vegetables and a creamy, sweet, salty and spicy peanut sauce…..yummola!

serves 6 (vegan)

noodles:

1 stick celery, cut into matchsticks

1 medium carrot, peeled and cut into matchsticks

1 red bell pepper (capsicum), seeded and cut into matchsticks

1 cup snow peas, cut into matchsticks

1 pound (450 g) Chinese egg noodles or thin spaghetti

¼ cup sesame seeds, toasted

¼ cup cilantro (coriander leaves)

dressing:

1 tablespoon sriracha chili sauce or sambal oelek

½ cup peanut butter

2 tablespoons toasted sesame oil

1 tablespoon brown sugar

3 tablespoons soy sauce

3 tablespoon rice vinegar

2 teaspoons fresh ginger, minced

1/2 cup water

salt to taste

Mix the dressing ingredients together.
Bring a large pot of salted water to a boil and cook the noodles until tender. Rinse under cold water and drain well. In a separate small saucepan, bring water to a boil. Blanch the carrots and snow peas briefly until crisp tender, drain and place in ice water for a few minutes, then drain thoroughly.

Mix everything together and garnish with sesame seeds and cilantro.

After the dressing has been mixed through the noodles, it is best to serve immediately.

watercress, jicama and orange salad with cilantro-lime dressing, pg 101

watercress, jicama and orange salad with cilantro-lime dressing

serves 4 (vegan)

2 bunches watercress

1½ cups jicama, cut into ¼-inch (0.6 cm) julienne

3 navel oranges

dressing:

½ cup cilantro (coriander leaves), chopped roughly

¼ cup lime juice (about 2 limes)

2 tablespoons rice wine vinegar

1 teaspoon lime zest

1 jalapeño chili

2 tablespoons (French) shallot, chopped roughly

2 tablespoons honey

1 teaspoon salt

¼ cup mild flavored oil, such as grapeseed oil (not olive oil)

Place dressing ingredients in a blender or use an immersion blender and blend until smooth. Cut the peel and all white pith off of the oranges. Using a sharp knife, cut segments from the orange, leaving the white membranes behind. Cut the segments in half and set aside. Remove the stems from the watercress, wash and spin dry. Mix with the watercress and jicama, pour over about ⅓ cup of dressing and toss gently. Taste and add more dressing if desired.

quinoa salad with asparagus, fava beans, garden peas, mint and feta

serves 4-6

1 cup quinoa, rinsed and drained

1½ cups vegetable stock

½ teaspoon salt

1 bunch asparagus

1 cup fresh fava or baby lima beans

1 cup garden peas

1 cup mint leaves, coarsely chopped

8 ounces (225 g) feta cheese, broken into approximately ½-inch (1.25 cm) chunks

dressing:

zest of 1 lemon

¼ cup lemon juice

1 tablespoon white balsamic or white wine vinegar

1 clove garlic, minced

¼ cup extra virgin olive oil

½ teaspoon salt

freshly ground black pepper

Heat 1½ cups stock and salt in a small saucepan, add the quinoa and bring to a boil. Cover, reduce to very low heat and cook for 18 minutes. Leave the lid on for 10 minutes before uncovering. Turn out into a large bowl, spreading out to cool. Set aside.

Continued on next page

Cut 2 inches (5 cm) from the bottom of asparagus stems and discard. Cut the asparagus into 1-inch (2.5 cm) lengths on a diagonal. Set aside.

Heat water in a large pot and cook the fava or lima beans for 1 minute. Remove with a slotted spoon, place in an ice bath for a few minutes and remove. Cook the peas according to directions if using frozen. Place in the ice bath for a few minutes, then drain. Add salt to the boiling water, then cook the asparagus until crisp tender, remove, place in the ice bath for a few minutes and drain.

Remove the skins from fava beans (if using) and set them aside. Mix together the dressing ingredients.
Toss the vegetables, mint and feta into the quinoa. Pour over the dressing and mix well. Serve immediately.

N.B. The salad can be made ahead of time. Add the dressing just before serving so the green vegetables retain their vibrant color.

endive and radicchio salad with apricots, toasted almonds and goat cheese

serves 4-6

4 large Belgian endives

1 head radicchio Treviso*

4 ripe apricots, halved, pitted and cut into ¼-inch (0.6 cm) wedges*

⅓ cup flaked almonds, toasted

4 ounces (110 g) soft goat cheese

dressing:

1½ tablespoons (French) shallots, chopped finely

1 tablespoon sherry vinegar

1 tablespoon aged balsamic vinegar

¼ teaspoon salt

¼ teaspoon freshly ground black pepper

3 tablespoons extra virgin olive oil

Whisk the dressing ingredients together. Cut the endives into quarters lengthwise, cut out and discard the cores. Tear the endive leaves into large pieces and place in a bowl. Cut the bottom quarter off the radicchio (removing the white part) and discard. Tear the leaves into large pieces and place in the bowl with the endive. Add the apricots to bowl. Drizzle over the dressing and toss to coat the leaves. Crumble goat cheese on top of the salad, sprinkle with toasted almonds and serve.

*radicchio Treviso is shaped like a small romaine/cos lettuce. If you can only find the round variety, that's fine you will just need less. (about half of a small one).

*apricots have a very short season during the Summer. As an alternative use dried apricots (not unsluphured). They should be bright orange and tart. Bring 1 cup of water to a boil and add ½ cup dried apricots. Turn off heat, cover and leave to soften for several hours. Drain and chop into ¼ inch dice.

arugula salad with muscat grapes, toasted almonds and manchego

serves 8-10

An adapation of a recipe by Suzanne Goin. This is a fantastic recipe; every ingredient marries perfectly together. Balsamic vinegar aged 12-15 years is key. Alternately, you can make a reduction yourself which is comparable (see pg 126).

½ pound (225 g) Muscat grapes or red grapes

½ cup flaked almonds, toasted

¼ pound (110 g) manchego cheese

½ pound (225 g) arugula

aged balsamic for drizzling

dressing:

1 tablespoon (French) shallots, minced

1 tablespoons sherry vinegar

1 tablespoon honey

¼ cup olive oil

1 tablespoon aged balsamic vinegar

½ teaspoon salt

freshly ground black pepper

Wash and cut the grapes in half and set aside. Shave the manchego cheese with a peeler. Whisk the dressing ingredients together. In a large bowl, add the arugula, grapes and toasted almonds. Drizzle with the vinaigrette and toss to coat. Arrange the salad on plates, scatter with the cheese, drizzle with aged balsamic vinegar and serve.

sweets

almond, date and lemon custard tart

Almond custard, dates and a hint of lemon in a buttery almond crust.

Fresh almond milk is deliciously nutty and creamy unlike its commercial counterpart found in supermarkets, and makes a great custard. If you are short on time you could Just make the filling and serve in small bowls dusted with cinnamon and powdered sugar. (although the combination of the crust and custard make it well worth the effort.)

makes one 9" tart (vegan)

1 x sweet tart shell see basic recipes

almond custard:

1 cup raw almonds

2½ cups water

2½ tablespoons cornstarch (cornflour)

1/3 cup white sugar

1 teaspoon lemon zest

½ teaspoon almond (essence)

½ teaspoon vanilla extract (essence)

1/2 teaspoon agar-agar powder* (see sources)

1 cup chopped seedless dates

¼ teaspoon salt

1½ teaspoons lemon juice

1 tablespoon powdered sugar

½ teaspoon ground cinnamon

Prepare fully baked sweet tart crust and set aside to cool.

Place the almonds in a saucepan with enough water to cover, then bring to a boil. Turn off the heat and leave for 2 minutes, then drain and run under cold water. Pinch off the skins, then place the almonds in a blender with the water. Blend on high speed for several minutes until almonds become a very fine meal. Strain through muslin cloth and squeeze well to remove as much milk as possible.

Pour ¼ cup of almond milk into a small bowl along with the cornstarch and whisk together. Pour into a heavy-bottomed saucepan along with the remaining almond milk, sugar, lemon zest, almond and vanilla essence and agar-agar. Bring to a boil, whisking constantly so lumps do not form, until the almond milk thickens. Add the salt and dates and simmer gently for 5 minutes. Add the lemon juice and mix well. Pour into the fully baked and cooled tart shell

Leave at room temperature for 30 minutes, then refrigerate for a minimum of an hour before serving. Mix the powdered sugar and cinnamon together and place in a fine-mesh sieve. Dust over the surface of the tart and serve.

*Agar-agar comes in flakes and a fine powder. If you can only find flakes, grind them in a coffee grinder until they become a fine powder.

apple bread and butter pudding

I have fond memories of growing up in Sydney and having fresh milk in glass bottles delivered to our home twice a week by the 'milko'. When we had an oversupply in the fridge, mum would ask me to make bread and butter pudding when I returned home from school. The recipe back then was an old-fashioned English/Aussie recipe. Buttered slices of bread in a baking dish were covered with a mixture of milk, egg and sugar, then finished off with a generous grating of nutmeg. Here is a more contemporary version that has become my favorite.

serves 6

4 tablespoons unsalted butter

½ cup brown sugar

2 apples, peeled, quartered and thinly sliced

⅓ cup dried currants

½ teaspoon ground cinnamon

¼ teaspoon ground nutmeg

3 eggs

1 cup whole milk

1 cup heavy (double) cream

¼ teaspoon salt

2 tablespoons white sugar

8 slices of brioche bread, crust removed

Heat oven to 350°F (175°C)
Melt the butter in a large frying pan. Add the brown sugar, apples, currants, cinnamon and nutmeg and mix well. Cook over low heat, stirring gently, for 5 minutes, then set aside. In a large bowl, mix together the eggs, milk, cream, salt and 2 tablespoons sugar.

Cut each slice of bread into approximately 8 pieces and gently mix with the apples and milk mixture.

Butter an 8" x 8" (20 cm x 20 cm) baking dish and pour in the bread mix.

Leave for 15 minutes to allow the bread to soak up the liquid. With the back of a wooden spoon, push the bread down into the liquid. Create a bain-marie by placing the pudding pan in a larger baking pan. Fill the outside pan with hot water to come halfway up the side of the pudding. Bake in the oven for 35-40 minutes. Cool for 10 minutes before serving.

mums's apricot nut bread, pg 109

mum's apricot nut bread

My mother used to make this every other week when I was growing up. It was a standard in our school lunch boxes, filled with tangy apricots, sweet raisins and crunchy walnuts. Serve it sliced with lashings of cold butter!

serves 10-12

8 ounces (225 g) dried apricots

2½ cups all-purpose (plain) flour

2 ounces (60 g) unsalted butter

2½ teaspoons baking powder

½ teaspoon salt

1 cup raisins (sultanas)

1 cup walnuts or pecans, chopped roughly

1 egg

1 cup white sugar

½ cup freshly squeezed orange juice

½ cup milk

¼ teaspoon baking soda (bicarbonate)

1 teaspoon vanilla extract (essence)

Heat the oven to 350°F (175°C)
Soak the dried apricots in boiling water for 30 minutes. Drain and chop roughly.
Sift the flour, baking powder and salt together. Rub the butter into the flour. Add the apricots, raisins and walnuts. Beat together the egg and sugar. Mix the baking soda and milk together, then add to the egg mix along with the orange juice and vanilla extract. Add the liquid ingredients to the flour and mix together quickly and lightly. Place in a well-greased 9-inch (22.5 cm) loaf pan and bake for 1¼ to 1½ hours.

banana tarte tatin with rum whipped cream

serves 6

⅔ cup superfine (caster) sugar*

zest of 1 orange

2 ounces (60 g) unsalted butter, chopped

pinch of salt

4 large firm, ripe bananas

1 sheet puff pastry, just thawed

1 cup cold heavy (double) cream

3 tablespoons confectioner's (icing) sugar

½ teaspoon vanilla extract (essence)

1-2 tablespoons dark rum

Preheat oven to 400°F (200°C)
Sprinkle the sugar evenly over the base of an 11-inch (28 cm) ovenproof frying pan. Place the frying pan over medium heat and cook the sugar and butter. From time to time, swirl the pan around to distribute the caramel and cook until the mixture becomes a deep golden brown, 8-10 minutes.
Remove from the heat and add the salt and orange zest.

Peel and cut the bananas in half crosswise, then in half lengthwise. Lay the bananas on the caramel, cut side up, in concentric circles beginning from the outside and working your way in. You will need to cut the bananas smaller to cover the center.

Continued on next page

Roll out the pastry to about ⅛ inch (0.3 cm) thickness. Cut the pastry into a circle an inch (2.5 cm) or so larger than the pan you are using; a dinner plate works well as a cutting guide. Gently lay the pastry over the bananas, tucking in the pastry between the rim of the pan and the edge of the bananas. Prick the pastry evenly over the surface in 8 places with a fork. Bake for 30 minutes, or until the pastry is golden brown and puffed and the caramel is bubbling around the sides. Remove from oven and rest for 2 minutes; no longer, or the caramel won't release.

Run a heat-proof spatula gently around the edges of the pastry to release it from the pan. Place a large plate over the pan and, using both hands (in oven mitts), clamp down both sides of the plate over the pan. Carefully and quickly turn the pan over, allowing the tart to release onto the plate. Serve hot or at room temperature with rum whipped cream (recipe below).

rum whipped cream: whip the cream in a bowl of an electric mixer fitted with a whisk attachment. When it starts to thicken, add the sugar, vanilla extract and rum, and continue to whip until it forms stiff peaks.

mango and passion fruit meringue roulade with raspberry sauce

Passion fruit, so tangy and fragrant. If you are unfamiliar with this fruit, it needs to mature to become sweet. The smooth purple orbs aren't really ready to eat until they begin to age and have a crinkly skin. If you have difficulty finding this fruit, the sweetness of the meringue is complemented well with other fruits that have a nice tang to them, so this recipe also works well with strawberries.

serves 6

roulade:

4 large egg whites, room temperature

1 cup superfine (caster) sugar

1 teaspoon cornstarch (cornflour)

1 teaspoon white vinegar

1 teaspoon vanilla extract (essence)

1½ cups heavy (double) cream

2 cups mango, peeled and cut into ½-inch (1.25 cm) dice, about 2-3 mangoes

6 passion fruits, pulped (see sources)

raspberry sauce:

8 ounces (225 g) frozen rasperries, thawed

2 tablespoons confectioner's (icing) sugar

roulade: Preheat the oven to 300°F (150°C). Line the base and sides of a 13x9 inch (33 x 23 cm) Swiss roll pan (tin) with parchment (non-stick) paper. Snip the corners of parchment diagonally to fit neatly.

Beat the egg whites with an electric mixer with whisk attachment until frothy, doubled in size, and soft peaks form. Slowly whisk in the sugar a tablespoon at a time until thick and shiny. Mix the cornstarch, vinegar and vanilla extract together, then whisk into egg whites.

Spoon into the pan and level carefully with a spatula, taking care not to push air from the egg whites. Bake for 30 minutes until the meringue surface is just firm.

sauce: Place the raspberries and sugar in a blender and blend until smooth, then push through a sieve. Refrigerate until ready to serve.

Continued on next page

Place a dishtowel (tea towel) onto a work surface and cover with a sheet of parchment (non-stick baking) paper and sprinkle with a little superfine (caster) sugar. Invert the hot meringue onto the paper and remove the pan. Leave to cool for about an hour. Remove the paper and spread whipped cream evenly over the meringue. Scatter the mango and passion fruit over the whipped cream. Use the paper to roll up the roulade from one short end, ending with the join underneath. Serve with raspberry sauce.

N.B. can be kept in the fridge for up to 2 days

prune flan

serves 4-6

Known in France as *far breton*. A custardy cake from Brittany, studded with brandy- or rum-soaked prunes. The texture is reminiscent of clafoutis, though even better in my opinion. This has to be the easiest dessert ever to make, and it's perfect for entertaining when you don't have a lot of time. If you aren't a fan of prunes, raisins (sultanas) work just as well.

¾ cup all-purpose (plain) flour

½ cup white sugar

2½ cups milk

4 ounces (110 g) unsalted butter, melted

3 eggs, slightly beaten

¼ teaspoon vanilla extract (essence)

⅛ teaspoon salt

9 ounces (250 g) prunes

½ cup brandy, Cognac or dark rum

confectioner's (icing) sugar for dusting

Soak the prunes in the liquor for several hours or overnight.

Whisk the melted butter, eggs, vanilla, sugar and about half the milk together. Add the flour and whisk briefly to incorporate. Pour into a bowl and mix in the remaining milk. Allow to rest for an hour or overnight in the refrigerator. Heat oven to 350°F (175°C).

Generously grease an 8"x8" (20 x 20 cm) oven-proof dish with softened butter.
Cover the bottom of dish with the prunes and their soaking liquid, then pour the batter over the prunes. Bake for 1 hour or until a knife inserted in the center comes out clean. Allow to cool for several hours, then dust with confectioner's sugar. Serve re-warmed or at room temperature.

pear, fresh ginger and date crumble

Fruit crumbles are the easiest desserts you can make. When I have friends coming over or need to take something along to a pot-luck gathering, fruit crumbles are the way to go! This recipe is great for autumn or winter when pears are in season.

serves 6-8

2½ pounds (1.1 kg) ripe pears, peeled, cored, quartered and cut into ½-inch (1.25 cm) dice

1 tablespoon lemon juice

1 cup + 1 tablespoon all-purpose (plain) flour, divided

2 tablespoons minced fresh ginger

2 tablespoons white sugar

½ teaspoon ground cinnamon

½ teaspoon ground cardamom

1 cup brown sugar

4 ounces (115 g) cold unsalted butter, chopped

1½ cups quick-cooking oatmeal

Heat the oven to 350°F (175°C)
In a large bowl mix together the pears, lemon juice, ginger, sugar, 1 tablespoon of flour and cinnamon. Place in a 10" x 8" (25 x 20 cm) oven-proof dish.

In a food processor, place 1 cup of flour and the brown sugar and pulse to mix together. Add the butter and process until it begins to clump together, about 30 seconds. Add the oatmeal and pulse a few times until combined. Spread over the top of the pears, then bake for approximately 45 minutes or until golden brown.

greta anna's plum cake

A wonderful recipe from the "Greta Anna Cookbook" that my mother has been making for over 20 years when plums are in season. A dry variety of plum works best so the fruit doesn't sink to the bottom of the cake. (Some of the Japanese varieties of plums, when ripe, can be overly juicy for this recipe.)

1 pound (450 g) plums, sliced thinly

7 ounces (200 g) unsalted butter, at room temperature

10½ tablespoons white sugar, divided

½ cup milk

2 eggs

grated zest of 1 lemon

1¾ cup self-rising flour

1 teaspoon baking powder

Heat the oven to 350°F (175°C).

Place the plums in a bowl, sprinkle with 3-4 tablespoons of sugar, and set aside. Sift the flour, salt and baking powder together.

Cream the butter with 4½ tablespoons sugar until the mixture is light and creamy. Add the eggs one at a time, beating well between each addition. Add the lemon zest, then on low speed alternate adding the milk with the flour.

Pour the batter into a buttered 10" (25 cm) springform pan. Drain the plums well, then place them evenly over the batter and sprinkle the remaining 2 tablespoons sugar all over the plums.

Bake for approximately 45-50 minutes, or until a skewer inserted in the center of the cake comes out clean.

gevulde speculaas

serves 12-16

Speculaas is an almond spice butter cookie that marks the arrival of Saint Nicholas Day in the Netherlands. It heralds the start of the holiday season. On the night of December 5th, Saint Nicholas visits homes and leaves gifts of fruit, nuts and cookies for good children in wooden clogs left by the fireplace. Gevulde speculaas translates as filled biscuit. The pastry is laced with aromatic spices and the center is home-made marzipan. This is an adaptation of my Dutch grandmother's recipe.

pastry:

2 cups all purpose (plain) flour

½ teaspoon salt

1½ teaspoons baking powder

spice mix (see below)

1 cup packed brown sugar

5 ounces (150 g) unsalted butter

3 tablespoons milk

2 egg yolks (reserve whites for almond paste)

spice mix:

4 teaspoon ground cinnamon

1 teaspoon ground nutmeg

1 teaspoon ground cloves

½ teaspoon ground white pepper

½ teaspoon ground ginger

½ teaspoon ground cardamom

marzipan:

12 ounces (340 g) ground almonds

2¼ cups white sugar

3 egg whites, lightly beaten

1½ tablespoons almond extract (essence)

zest of 1 orange

to finish:

2 ounces (60 g) flaked or slivered almonds

pastry: Mix the flour, spices, brown sugar, and salt together, then rub in butter until it is the consistency of damp sand. This can all be done in a food processor. Whisk the egg yolks and milk together in a separate bowl. Empty the flour into a bowl, then add only enough milk-egg mix to make it into a cohesive ball with your hands without being sticky. Knead the dough lightly. Reserve remaining liquid for final egg-wash.

Divide the dough in half and press into flat discs. Wrap the two pieces separately in plastic wrap and chill in the refrigerator for several hours, or preferably overnight.

marzipan: Mix the almonds, sugar, zest and almond extract. Add the egg white and mix well until it holds together.

assembly: Roll out both portions of pastry on parchment (non-stick baking) paper to ⅛ inch (0.3 cm) thick, then line a 9-inch (22.5 cm) tart pan with removable bottom with one portion. Remove any excess pastry from the sides. Pat the marzipan into a disc the width of the tart pan. Press evenly into the pan. Place the remaining pastry over the almond meal. Remove excess pastry from the edges.

Brush the surface with the reserved egg-milk mix. Scatter the surface with the flaked almonds and press them gently onto the pastry. Bake in a 300°F (150°C) oven for approximately 45 minutes, or until tart has risen and is golden brown. Cool for several hours on a wire rack, then cut into 12 slices.

black sticky rice pudding with banana & coconut milk

serves 4

A classic Southeast Asian dessert which has a wonderful texture and flavor. The sweetened black rice is beautifully complimented by the slightly salty coconut milk. Black glutinous rice can be readily found in Asian food markets.

1½ cups black glutinous rice, washed and soaked overnight

¼ cup palm sugar (or brown sugar)

¼ cup white sugar

2 pandan leaves or 1 teaspoon pandan extract (essence) (optional, see sources)

1 cup coconut milk

¼ teaspoon salt

1 tablespoon unsalted butter

2 ripe bananas

2 tablespoons toasted sesame seeds

rice: Drain the rice. Combine with the sugar, 1 pandan leaf and 4 cups of water in a pressure cooker and cook for 20-25 minutes. [Stove top method: Simmer uncovered for 60 minutes with 6 cups water. Add more water if needed.] When cooked, the grains should be soft and the finished consistency should be like a soft pudding.

coconut sauce: Combine the coconut milk and salt in a saucepan. Bring to a boil, then remove from the heat. Slice the bananas ½ inch (1.25 cm) thick on the diagonal. Heat the butter in a non-stick pan and sear the bananas until golden brown.

Serve the rice warm in bowls with coconut sauce on top. Garnish with bananas and sprinkle with sesame seeds.

fresh ginger cakes with ginger crème anglaise and poached pear

serves 6-7

An adaptation of a recipe from David Lebovitz, these are baked in ramekins, then turned out and served with crème anglaise and a fan of pear. If you would prefer to make it as a whole cake, like the original recipe, double the recipe and bake in a 9" x 13" (22.5 x 32.5 cm) parchment-lined pan for 1 hour, then cool in the pan for 30 minutes before turning out.

individual cakes:

2 ounces (60 g) fresh ginger

½ cup mild (non-blackstrap) molasses

½ cup white sugar

½ cup vegetable oil, preferably peanut

2½ cups all-purpose (plain) flour

½ teaspoon ground cinnamon

¼ teaspoon ground cloves

¼ teaspoon freshly ground black pepper

½ cup water

1 teaspoon baking soda (bicarbonate)

1 egg, at room temperature

poached pears:

3 ripe but firm Bosc pears

1 cup white sugar

1 quart (1 L) water

2 cinnamon sticks

2 cloves

ginger crème anglaise:

2 cups (475 ml) whole milk

1¼ inch (3 cm) chunk of fresh ginger, 1½ inches (3.8 cm) in diameter

1 teaspoon vanilla extract (essence)

4 egg yolks

½ cup white sugar

cakes: Position the oven rack in the center of the oven. Preheat the oven to 350°F (175°C). Line the bottom of 7 ramekins (1-cup size) with parchment paper. Peel, slice, and chop the ginger very fine with a knife, or use a grater. Mix together the molasses, sugar, and oil. In another bowl, sift together the flour, cinnamon, cloves and black pepper

Bring the water to a boil in a saucepan, stir in the baking soda, and then mix the hot water into the molasses mixture. Stir in the ginger. Gradually whisk the dry ingredients into the batter. Add the egg, and continue mixing until everything is thoroughly combined. Pour the batter into the prepared ramekins so they are only ¾ filled and bake for about 30 minutes, until the top of the cakes spring back lightly when pressed or a toothpick inserted into the center comes out clean.

Cool the cakes for at least 30 minutes. Run a knife around the edge of the cake to loosen it from the ramekin. Remove the cakes from the ramekins and peel off the parchment paper.

pears: In a large saucepan, heat the water and sugar until sugar is dissolved. Add the cinnamon and cloves. Peel, halve and core the pears using a melon baller or teaspoon and add the pears to poaching liquid. Make sure your saucepan is big enough to comfortably fit the pears so they are submerged in liquid.

Continued on next page

115

Simmer gently until pears are cooked through, about 15-25 minutes. Remove the pears carefully with a slotted spoon and set aside. Increase the heat and reduce the poaching liquid until it becomes syrupy. Remove the spices and return the pears to saucepan.

crème anglaise: Pour the milk into a saucepan large enough to hold all the ingredients. Slice the ginger into ¼-inch (0.6 cm) coins, add to the milk and bring to a simmer. Remove from the heat and stir in the vanilla. Whisk the egg yolks and sugar together in a bowl until they are pale yellow and fall from the whisk in ribbons.

Slowly whisk the warm milk into the egg mixture. Pour the mixture back into the saucepan and return to the stove over medium-low heat. Stir continuously with a wooden spoon for about 5 to 7 minutes or until the mixture has thickened just slightly. Do not boil, or it will curdle. The custard is ready when you lift the spoon out, draw your finger down the back of the spoon and the line doesn't fill in. Quickly pour the crème anglaise through a fine sieve into the bowl and press plastic wrap onto the surface so a skin doesn't form.

N.B. If the custard overcooks and turns grainy, remove it from the heat, take out the vanilla bean, add 2 tablespoons of cold cream and mix in an electric blender until smooth. Then proceed with the recipe.

to serve: Place the pears on a cutting board and use a sharp knife to cut them in half. Slice the pears at ¼-inch (0.6 cm) intervals lengthwise, leaving intact the top ¼ inch (0.6 cm). Gently spread the sliced pear quarters until slightly fanned. On individual plates pour about ¼ cup or less of crème anglaise, place the cake in center then place a fanned pear on top of the cake. Dust lightly with cinnamon (optional) and serve.

rhubarb and buttermilk custard tart

Rhubarb and custard: for me this is a heavenly combination. The second time I tested this recipe, I thought I'd try a little vanilla extract and it really was not a good addition (in case you are tempted to try this). The vanilla masks the delicate flavor of the buttermilk.

1 pound (450 g) rhubarb, cut into 1 inch (2.5 cm) lengths

3 tablespoons superfine (caster) sugar

2 tablespoons all-purpose (plain) flour

1 cup buttermilk

¾ cup white sugar

3 large eggs

2 tablespoons unsalted butter, melted

short crust pastry, par-baked (see basic recipes)

Preheat the oven to 400°F (200°C). Toss the rhubarb with 3 tablespoons sugar and bake for 15 minutes or until tender. Set aside to cool. Place the baked rhubarb in a bowl and gently fold in the flour. Spread the rhubarb evenly over the base of the par-baked tart shell. In a bowl whisk together the eggs, buttermilk, butter and sugar and pour over the rhubarb. Reduce the oven to 350°F (175°C) and bake the tart for 40 minutes or until the custard is set.

ricotta, orange and chocolate budino

Essentially a baked ricotta flan with the classic flavors of the Sicilian dessert, cassata. Creamy ricotta, orange, raisins, rum and chocolate, a magical combo. This budino needs several hours in the fridge to set after baking, so you may want to make this the day before serving.

Makes 5

2½ tablespoons dark rum

½ cup raisins (sultanas)

½ cup candied orange peel, chopped roughly

⅔ cup white sugar

2 egg yolks

1 whole egg

1 pound (450 g) good quality ricotta, drained

½ cup heavy (double) cream

½ teaspoon almond extract (essence)

pinch salt

unsweetened cocoa powder for dusting

oven-proof ramekins (1-cup size)

Preheat the oven to 325°F (165°C).

Soak the raisins and orange peel in rum and set aside for an hour. In a mixing bowl, whisk together the eggs, sugar, ricotta, cream, almond extract and salt. Add the rum-soaked fruit including the soaking liquid to the bowl, mix, and scrape into a blender. Blend until smooth, about 1 minute.

Place the ramekins in a baking dish. Use a ladle to fill with the ricotta mix. Pour boiling water into the baking dish until it comes halfway up the sides of the ramekins. Cover the baking dish with aluminum foil and bake in the oven until the centers are still soft and jiggly when you tap the cups, 50-60 minutes. Transfer the ramekins to a rack to cool. Cover with plastic wrap and refrigerate for several hours or overnight.

Dust generously with cocoa powder just before serving.

flourless orange and almond cake

Ground almonds replace flour in this recipe and give the cake a delightful moist and nutty texture. It is then finished with a zesty orange syrup.

serves 12 (gluten free)

cake:

melted unsalted butter, for greasing

2 oranges, preferably navel

3 eggs

1 cup superfine (caster) sugar

3 cups ground almonds

1 teaspoon baking powder

orange syrup:

1 orange

¾ cup white sugar

Preheat oven to 340°F (170°C). Brush a round 8" (22.5 cm) springform pan (tin) with the melted butter. Line the base with non-stick baking (parchment) paper.

Place the oranges in a saucepan and cover with cold water. Bring to a boil over medium heat. Cook for 15 minutes or until tender. Drain. Return to the pan and cover with cold water. Bring to a boil and cook for 15 minutes (this will reduce the bitterness of the peel). Refresh under cold water and drain. Coarsely chop the oranges. Remove and discard seeds if any. Place the oranges in the bowl of a food processor and process until smooth.

Use an electric beater to whisk the eggs and sugar in a bowl until thick and pale. Add the oranges, almond meal and baking powder, and gently fold by hand until just combined. Pour into the prepared pan.

Bake for 1 hour or until a skewer inserted into the center comes out clean. Cool for 15 minutes.

orange syrup: use a zester to remove the rind from the orange, then juice the orange.

Place the rind in a saucepan of boiling water and cook for 5 minutes, or until soft. Drain the water and discard. Return to pan with the orange juice and sugar. Place over low heat and cook, stirring, for 2-3 minutes, or until the sugar dissolves and the syrup thickens.

Turn the cake onto a serving plate. Use a skewer to gently prick the top. Spoon over the syrup. Cut into wedges to serve.

ricotta, chocolate and orange budino, pg 117

the basics

ingredients, techniques and basic recipes

salt

I highly recommend using a good quality 100% natural sea salt. Common table salt highly refined and often includes added iodine and chemicals. Best to avoid it all together. Good-quality salt improves the taste of your food and is better for you.

quick vegetable stock

Not everyone has time to make vegetable stock. If you want a simple alternative, I suggest a good quality vegetable bouillon (see sources). Bouillons contain a fair amount of salt, so use sparingly, and use before you add any additional salt to the recipe. Liquid stocks in Tetra-packs are not a good alternative and can potentially change the flavor of your dish adversely.

oils

Use good quality *cold-pressed extra-virgin olive oil.* If the label doesn't say extra virgin, it has been refined. Many olive oils are blends from different estates, which is less expensive and fine for cooking. Single-origin olive oils are a good choice for salads and dishes where you would use oil to flavor or finish a dish.
Grapeseed oil has a neutral taste which I prefer to use in Asian and Indian cooking. It has a high smoke point, so it is perfect for stir-frying etc.
Safflower oil is a good alternative. I tend to stay away from canola (rapeseed) oil, as it is genetically engineered.

butter

Unsalted butter is always used for baking and I prefer to use it for general cooking. Salted butter can add additional salt to your cooking, which could interfere with the overall salty flavor of your dish. Unsalted butter is generally considered to be of fresher, better quality than salted butter, as it doesn't have the addition of salt to preserve it for a longer shelf life.

fresh herbs

I prefer to use fresh herbs whenever possible, as they do have a fresher, more herbal flavor. If you use dried herbs, which are more concentrated, use ⅓ of the fresh quantity.

spices and dried herbs

Ground spices tend to lose their flavor after 6-9 months once opened. If the containers are unopened, they can last 2-3 years. Whole spices such as cinnamon sticks and peppercorns have a longer shelf life, up to two years. Store your spices in a cool dark place for maximum shelf life, and date them once opened. You may want to invest in a spice or coffee grinder if you don't already have one, and grind your spices such as coriander seed, cumin, cardamon etc fresh, in small quantities, for maximum flavor and freshness.

tofu

Available in many forms, i.e., silken, soft and firm.
If a recipe calls for pressed tofu, rinse the tofu, pat dry then wrap in 3 layers of paper towel. Place a plate and a weight on top. Leave the tofu for 20 minutes before proceeding with the recipe.

cleaning artichokes

1. Using a serrated knife, cut off the spiky top third of a baby artichoke and discard the trimmings.

2. Pull back each dark outer leaf and snap it off at the base until you reach the tender, pale green inner leaves.

3. Use a vegetable peeler to remove the tough outer layers around the stem until you reach the pale layer underneath.

4. Leave the stem attached. With a paring knife, cut off the bottom ¼ inch (0.6 cm) of the stem.

5. Cut the artichokes into quarters and submerge in a bowl of water with the juice of 2 lemons until ready to use.

peeling tomatoes

Bring enough water to a boil to submerge the tomatoes required for recipe. With a small, sharp knife, cut out the stem end of tomatoes, then cut a shallow X at the other end. Submerge the tomatoes for 10-15 seconds, then remove with tongs and place in an ice bath or in a bowl of running water. If you need to peel more than 3 tomatoes, you may need to work in batches.

basic vegetable stock

makes approx 1 quart (1 litre)

Make a double batch and freeze what's left over so you have it on hand when you need it in a pinch. I add a minimal amount of salt in my stock, so it doesn't interfere with the salt quantities I have written into my recipes. Regardless, it is always best to taste what you are cooking before adding salt, then add salt if needed.

2 tablespoons olive oil

1 large onion, chopped roughly

3 large carrots, chopped roughly

2 stalks celery, chopped roughly

1 small leek, washed very well and chopped roughly

2 cloves garlic

6 black peppercorns

1 sprig thyme

1 small bay leaf

1 teaspoon salt

6½ cups water

Heat the oil in a large, wide pot. Add the vegetables and garlic and cook over low heat for 5 minutes. Add the peppercorns, thyme, bay leaf, salt and water, and bring to a boil. Reduce the heat to very low and simmer the stock gently for 40 minutes, or until reduced by one third of original volume.

Strain the stock through a fine sieve and let cool. Cover and keep it in the refrigerator until needed, for a maximum of 1 week.

savory tart shell

makes enough for a 10-inch (25 cm) tart crust

2 cups all purpose (plain) flour

6 ounces (170 g) unsalted butter, cut into ½-inch (1.25 cm) dice

½ teaspoon salt

½ teaspoon sugar

6-7 tablespoons ice water

In a food processor add the flour, salt, suga and pulse a few times then and butter and process until the butter resembles pea-sized crumbs. Gradually add just enough ice water until it just begins to hold together. Turn dough out onto a lightly floured surface and very lightly knead together just to incorporate any dry ingredients. It should be moist but not sticky. Flatten into a disk about ½ inch (1.25 cm) thick. Wrap in plastic wrap and refrigerate for about an hour.

Oil a 10-inch (25 cm) fluted tart pan with a removable bottom.

Place the dough on a floured surface roll to ⅛ inch (0.3 cm) thickness. Place it in the tart shell and press it into the pan. Trim the overhang by ½ inch (1.25 cm) and fold it back into the sides of pan to make double-thick sides. Pierce the surface of the crust with a fork and place it in freezer for a minimum of ½ hour

To fully or partially bake the crust: Place a rack in the center of oven and preheat the oven to 375°F (190°C). Oil the shiny side of a piece of aluminum foil (or use nonstick foil) and fit the foil, oiled side down, tightly against the crust. Since you froze the crust, you can bake it without weights. Put the tart pan on a baking sheet and bake the crust for 20 to 25 minutes.

Carefully remove the foil. If the crust has puffed, press it down gently with the back of a spoon. Bake the crust for 5 minutes longer to partially bake. To bake fully, continue to bake until golden brown. Transfer the pan to a rack and cool the crust to room temperature, and proceed with the rest of your recipe.

sweet tart shell

An adaptation of a wonderful recipe from Dorie Greenspan which doesn't require 'pie weights'

makes enough for one 9-inch (22.5 cm) tart crust

1½ cups all-purpose (plain) flour

½ cup confectioner's (icing) sugar

¼ teaspoon salt

9 tablespoons very cold unsalted butter, cut into small pieces

1 egg

dough: Put the flour, confectioner's sugar and salt in the bowl of a food processor and pulse a couple of times to combine. Scatter the pieces of butter over the dry ingredients and pulse until the butter is cut in coarsely; you'll have some pieces the size of oatmeal flakes and some pea-size pieces.

Stir the egg yolk to break it up. Add it to the food processor a little at a time, pulsing after each addition. When the egg is in, pulse until the dough, which will look granular soon after the egg is added, forms clumps and curds. Just before you reach this clumpy stage, the sound of the machine working the dough will change—heads up! Turn the dough out onto a work surface.

Continued on next page

Very lightly and sparingly knead the dough just to incorporate any dry ingredients that might have escaped mixing. Gather the dough into a ball (you might have to use a little more pressure than you used to mix in the dry bits, because you do want the ball to be just barely cohesive), flatten it into a disk, wrap it well and chill it for at least 2 hours or for up to 1 day.

rolled-out crust: This dough is very soft - a combination of a substantial amount of butter and the use of confectioners' sugar - so it is easier to roll it between wax paper or plastic wrap. Roll the dough out evenly, turning the dough over frequently and lifting the wax paper or plastic wrap often, so that it doesn't roll into the dough and form creases. If you've got time, slide the rolled out dough into the fridge to rest and firm for about 20 minutes before fitting the dough into the buttered tart pan.
Turn to dough out into a tart pan and trim overhang to ½ inch then fold into sides to make double thick sides. Pierce base all over with a fork and Freeze the crust for at least 30 minutes, preferably longer, before baking.

To partially bake the crust: Place a rack in the center of the oven and preheat the oven to 375°F (190°C). Butter the shiny side of a piece of aluminum foil and fit the foil tightly against the crust. Bake the crust 25 minutes, then carefully remove the foil. If the crust has puffed, press it down gently with the back of a spoon. Bake for another 3 to 5 minutes, then transfer the crust to a cooling rack; keep it in its pan.

Fully baked crust: Continue to bake after the aluminum has been removed until golden brown.

vegan sweet tart shell

makes enough for one 9-inch (22.5 cm) tart crust

1½ cups all-purpose (plain) flour

¾ cup ground almonds

½ teaspoon salt

¼ cup confectioner's (icing) sugar

4 ounces (115 gms) vegan butter substitute, frozen

2 tablespoons ice water

dough: Put the flour, ground almonds, confectioner's sugar and salt in the bowl of a food processor and pulse a couple of times to combine. Scatter the pieces of butter over the dry ingredients and pulse until the butter is cut in coarsely; you'll have some pieces the size of oatmeal flakes and some pea-size pieces and that's just fine. Add water 1 tablespoons at a time pulsing after each addition. When the water is in, process in long pulses until the dough forms clumps. Just before it reaches this clumpy stage, the sound of the machine working the dough will change. Turn the dough out onto a work surface.

Follow on from the method of 'Sweet Tart Shell' to complete. Fully bake the crust and cool on rack in tart pan.

paneer

makes 12 ounces (340 g)

8 cups milk

¼ cup lemon juice

Line a colander with 2 layers of cheesecloth, draping it over the sides, and set it in a sink. Bring the milk to just under a boil in a 4-quart (4 L) saucepan over medium-high heat, stirring often with a wooden spoon to prevent it from scorching. Reduce the heat to medium-low, add the juice, and stir gently until large curds form, about 30 seconds. If it doesn't curdle, add another tablespoon of lemon juice. Pour the milk mixture into the colander. Gather the corners of cheesecloth together and gently squeeze out the liquid with the back of a wooden spoon.

Grab the ends of the cheesecloth and twist the ball of cheese to squeeze out the excess whey. (You many want to wear rubber gloves for this as it will be very hot). Tie the cheesecloth to your kitchen faucet and allow the cheese to drain for about 5 minutes. Twisting the ball to compact the cheese into a block, place it on a plate with the twisted part of the cheesecloth on the side and set another plate on top. Weigh the second plate down a heavy pot filled with cans of beans inside for extra weight. Move it to the refrigerator and let it sit about 20 minutes. Unwrap and cut into ½-inch (1.25 cm) cubes.

balsamic reduction

A traditionally aged balsamic vinegar known as saba, vin cotto or balsamico tradizionale can be very expensive, so I have provided a recipe to make a reduction comparable to saba using regular balsamic vinegar. Balsamic reductions are delicious over strawberries, peaches, pears and vegetables. Make this condiment a staple in your pantry!

makes 1/3 cup

2/3 cup balsamic vinegar

2 tablespoon white sugar

2 tablespoon port wine

Place all of the ingredients into a small heavy bottomed saucepan and cook over *very low* heat so it barely simmers. Continue to cook until it is reduced by half. Store in a glass container.

sources

Agar Agar
Health food stores
U.S.: Whole Foods Market
Asian food stores

Ancho chili powder
Mexican food stores
U.S.: Whole Foods Market
Australia: **www.fireworksfood.com.au**

Annatto/Achiote a seed that adds both color and flavor. Common to Latin American and Caribbean cuisine.
Whole Foods Market
Kalyustans (**www.kalyustans.com**), based in New York, ships throughout the U.S.
Latin food markets

Berbere a spice blend from Ethiopia
U.S.: Whole Foods Market
Gourmet food markets

Black mustard seeds (Rai)
Indian food stores

Chestnut flour
Whole Foods Market, Italian food markets, gourmet food stores. Store in the freezer.

Curry leaves (curry patta)
Indian food markets
Kalyustans (**www.kalyustans.com**), based in New York, ships throughout the U.S.

Five Spice Powder
U.S.: Whole Foods Market
gourmet food markets, Asian food markets

Fresh grated coconut
Indian and Asian food markets (freezer section)

Hoisin sauce
Asian food markets
Ethnic foods aisle of major supermarkets
U.S.: Whole Foods Market

Ketchap Manis is a sweet soy sauce from Indonesia and tastes quite different from 'Chinese sweet soy sauce'.
Asian food markets
U.S.: Kalyustans (**www.kalyustans.com**), based in NY, ships throughout the U.S.

Mirin Japanese sweet cooking wine
Asian food markets
U.S.: Whole Foods Market

Pandan leaves and extract (essence)
Asian food markets
Kalyustans (**www.kalyustans.com**), based in New York, ships throughout the U.S.
Leaves are often frozen.

Paneer Indian fresh pressed cheese.
Indian food markets
U.S.: Whole Foods Market

Passion fruit
Readily available in Australia and the Caribbean. N.Y.C.: (seasonal) Agata and Valentina, Dean & Deluca, Citarella, Whole Foods Market
U.S.: Amazon.com, "John West passion fruit pulp 170gm cans"

Pomegranate molasses
U.S.: Whole Foods Market
Kalyustans (**www.kalyustans.com**), based in New York, ships throughout the U.S.
Gourmet markets, Middle Eastern markets

Smoked tofu
U.S.: Whole Foods Market (SoyBoy brand)
Good health food stores

Tamarind concentrate
U.S.: Whole Foods Market
Asian/Indian food markets (see basic
ingredients)

Teff
A nutritious grain native to Ethiopia. Available
in health food stores.

Vegetable bouillon
U.S.: Whole Foods Market '"Better Than
Bouillon" (comes in a jar)
Australia: "Swiss Marigold Vegetable Bouillon"
available in health food stores

A

Apples
Apple bread and butter pudding, 107

Apricots
Endive and radicchio salad with apricots,
    toasted almonds and goat cheese, 102
Mum's apricot nut bread, 109

Artichokes
Braised favas, fennel and artichokes, 80

Asparagus
Quinoa salad with asparagus, fava beans,
    garden peas, mint and feta, 101
Stir-fried vegetables and tofu with orange-
    maple glaze, 39

Avocado
Butter lettuce with avocado, mango,
    cucumber, lime and sweet
    chili dressing, 93
Cheddar and mango quesadillas with
    guacamole, 34
Corn cakes with avocado and spicy tomato
    salsa, 6
Peruvian potato, cheese and avocado soup, 19

B

Bananas
Banana tarte tatin with rum whipped cream,
    107
Black sticky rice pudding with banana and
    coconut milk, 114

Beans, Lentils and Legumes
Braised favas, fennel and artichokes, 80
Brazilian black bean and sweet potato soup
    with mango, 13
Cannellini bean and kale soup, 14
Chickpea crepes with cilantro chutney, 7
Eggplant and lentil ragu, 38

Lentil and mushroom croquettes with
    roasted bell pepper gastrique, 76
Lentil and vegetable loaf with mushroom-
    rosemary au jus, 36
Moroccan braised vegetables with chickpeas
    and dates, 53
Pasta e fagioli with porcini mushrooms, 18
Quinoa salad with asparagus, fava beans,
    garden peas, mint and feta, 101
Red lentil, sweet potato and peanut soup
    with greens, 22
Rice and beans with smoked tofu sofrito, 41
Split pea and potato soup, 17
Vegetable and cannellini bean goulash with
    parsley dumplings, 60
Yellow split pea and spinach dhal, 21

Beets
Pumpernickel with roasted beets, goat cheese
    and pesto, 28
Roasted beet salad with beet greens, orzo
    pasta, feta and pine nuts, 92

Berries
Mango and passion fruit meringue roulade with
    raspberry sauce, 110
Swedish oatmeal pancakes with raspberry-
    cranberry compote, 2

Broccoli
Cold udon noodles with broccoli, tofu and
    pickled ginger, 95
Red lentil, sweet potato and peanut soup
    with greens, 22

Butternut squash
See Squash

C

Cabbage
Vegetable and cannellini bean goulash with
parsley dumplings, 60

Cakes and Sweet Breads
Flourless orange and almond cake, 118
Fresh ginger cakes with ginger crème anglaise
and poached pear, 115
Greta Anna's plum cake, 112
Gevulde speculass, 113
Mum's apricot nut bread, 109

Capsicums
See Peppers and Chilies

Carrots
Balsamic glazed carrots, 80
Braised carrots with tomato and thyme, 88
Moroccan braised vegetables with chickpeas
and dates, 53
Peanut sesame noodles, 99
Quinoa vegetable biryani, 85
Rice pilaf with carrots, currants, pine nuts
and dill, 86
Roasted bell pepper and carrot soup, 12
Tofu and vegetable bourguignon pie, 59
Vegetable and cannellini bean goulash with
parsley dumplings, 60

Cauliflower
Cauliflower and almond soup, 15
Quinoa vegetable biryani, 85
Quinoa with roasted cauliflower and olives, 84
Roasted cauliflower florets with porcini
mushroom and cheese crust, 89
Spaghetti with roasted cauliflower, raisins,
pine nuts and green olives, 46

Cheese
Arugula salad with muscat grapes,
toasted almonds and manchego, 103
Butternut squash and ricotta galette with
sage butter, 50

Cheddar and mango quesadillas with
guacamole, 34
Endive and radicchio salad with apricots,
toasted almonds and goat cheese, 102
Escarole, goat cheese, date and walnut salad
with pomegranate dressing, 97
Kale and feta pie with pine nuts and raisins, 33
Kale and paneer curry, 44
Pan-fried ricotta polenta with ratatouille, 73
Peruvian potato, cheese and avocado soup, 19
Portobello mushroom burgers with peperonata,
arugula pesto and mozzarella, 54
Portobello mushrooms filled with caramelized
onion, spinach, tomato and mozzarella, 43
Pumpernickel with roasted beets, goat cheese
and pesto, 28
Quinoa salad with asparagus, fava beans,
garden peas, mint and feta, 101
Radicchio and goat cheese crespelle with
parmesan besciamella, 64
Ricotta, orange and chocolate budino, 117
Roasted beet salad with beet greens,
orzo pasta, feta and pine nuts, 92
Roasted cauliflower florets with porcini
mushroom and cheese crust, 89
Roasted vegetable and cheese strudel
with tomato coulis, 70

Chickpeas
Chickpea crepes with cilantro chutney, 7
Moroccan braised vegetables with chickpeas
and dates, 53

Chilies
See Peppers and Chilies

Coconut
Vegetable kootu, 37

Corn
Corn cakes with avocado and spicy
tomato salsa, 6
Late summer harvest vegetable tart, 47

Sweet corn and miso soup, 16
Sweet corn fritters, 81

Crepes
Chickpea crepes with cilantro chutney, 7
Radicchio and goat cheese crespelle with
    parmesan besciamella, 64

Cucumber
Butter lettuce with avocado, mango, cucumber,
    lime and sweet chili dressing, 93

Currants
Kale salad with pine nuts, currants and shaved
    parmesan, 98
Rice pilaf with carrots, currants, pine nuts
    and dill, 86

D
Dates
Almond, date and lemon custard tart, 106
Escarole, goat cheese, date and walnut salad
    with pomegranate dressing, 97
Moroccan braised vegetables with chickpeas
    and dates, 53

E
Eggplant
Eggplant and lentil ragu, 38
Eggplant caponata stuffed eggs, 29
Malaysian-style vegetable and tofu curry, 52
Moroccan braised vegetables with chickpeas
    and dates, 53
Pan-fried ricotta polenta with ratatouille, 73
Ratatouille masala, 90
Roasted vegetable and cheese strudel with
    tomato coulis, 70
Winter vegetable and miso stew, 56

Eggs
Apple bread and butter pudding, 107
Black sticky rice pudding with banana
    and coconut milk, 114
Chestnut and almond waffles with maple
    poached pears, 10
Corn cakes, 6

Eggplant caponata stuffed eggs, 29
Flourless orange and almond cake, 118
Fresh ginger cakes with ginger crème anglaise
    and poached pear, 115
Gevulde speculaas, 113
Greta Anna's plum cake, 112
Grits with cheddar, spinach, tomato and
    poached eggs, 3
Kale and feta pie with pine nuts and raisins, 33
Late summer harvest vegetable tart, 47
Lentil and mushroom croquettes with
    red bell pepper gastrique, 76
Lentil and vegetable loaf with mushroom-
    rosemary au jus, 36
Masala scrambled egg wrap, 8
Mum's apricot nut bread, 109
Mushroom stroganov with teff spaetzle
    and sautéed tuscan kale, 77
Potato roesti with sautéed mushrooms,
    poached eggs and sauce meurette, 72
Prune flan, 111
Radicchio and goat cheese crespelle with
    parmesan besciamella, 64
Ricotta, orange and chocolate budino, 117
Roasted vegetable and cheese strudel with
    tomato coulis, 70
Shakshouka, 5
Swedish oatmeal pancakes with
    raspberry-cranberry compote, 2
Sweet corn fritters, 81
Tomato and tamarind egg curry, 42

F
Fennel
Braised favas, fennel and artichokes, 80
Fennel braised in orange juice, 88

Figs
Sautéed spinach with black mission figs, 83

G
Grains
Black sticky rice pudding with banana
    and coconut milk, 114

Mushroom stroganov with teff spaetzle
  and sautéed tuscan kale, 77
Quinoa pilaf, 84
Quinoa salad with asparagus, fava beans,
garden peas, mint and feta, 101
Quinoa vegetable biryani, 85
Quinoa with roasted cauliflower and olives, 84
Rice and beans with smoked tofu sofrito, 41
Rice pilaf with carrots, currants, pine nuts
  and dill, 86
Swedish oatmeal pancakes with
  raspberry-cranberry compote, 2

Grapes
Arugula salad with muscat grapes, toasted
  almonds and manchego, 103

Green Beans
Black pepper tofu and green beans, 49
Breen beans braised in tomato with cinnamon
  and allspice, 82
Malaysian-style vegetable and tofu curry, 52

Grits
See Polenta

J
Jicama
Watercress, jicama and orange salad with
  cilantro-lime dressing, 101

K
Kale
Bubble and squeak with pan-fried tofu and
  onion gravy, 32
Cannellini bean and kale soup, 14
Kale and feta pie with pine nuts and raisins, 33
Kale and paneer curry, 44
Kale salad with pine nuts, currants and shaved
  parmesan, 98
Mushroom stroganov with teff spaetzle
  and sautéed tuscan kale, 77
Sautéed kale with shiitake mushrooms, 83

L
Leeks
Curried potato and leek soup, 16

M
Mangos
Butter lettuce with avocado, mango, cucumber,
  lime and sweet chili dressing, 93
Cheddar and mango quesadillas
  with guacamole, 34
Mango and passion fruit meringue roulade
  with raspberry sauce, 110

Miso
Baby spinach and roasted butternut squash
  salad with miso dressing, 92
Sweet corn and miso soup, 16
Winter vegetable and miso stew, 56

Mushrooms
Arugula salad with sautéed mushrooms, pear,
  celery, walnuts and shaved parmesan, 97
Lentil and mushroom croquettes with roasted
  bell pepper gastrique, 76
Lentil and vegetable loaf with mushroom-
  rosemary au jus, 36
Masala scrambled egg wrap, 8
Mushroom stroganov with teff spaetzle
  and sautéed tuscan kale, 77
Portobello mushroom burgers with peperonata,
  arugula pesto and mozzarella, 54
Portobello mushrooms filled with caramelized
  onion, spinach, tomato and mozzarella, 43
Potato roesti with sautéed mushrooms,
  poached eggs and sauce meurette, 72
Roasted cauliflower florets with porcini
  mushroom and cheese crust, 89
Sautéed kale with shiitake mushrooms, 83
Strozzapreti with spinach sauce and sautéed
  mushrooms, 40
Tofu and vegetable bourguignon pie, 59
Vegetable and cannellini bean goulash with
  parsley dumplings, 60
Walnut and mushroom pâté, 27

N

Noodles

Cold udon noodles with broccoli, tofu and pickled ginger, 95

Peanut sesame noodles, 99

Nuts

Almond, date and lemon custard tart, 106

Arugula salad with muscat grapes, toasted almonds and manchego, 103

Arugula salad with sautéed mushrooms, pear, celery, walnuts and shaved parmesan, 97

Cauliflower and almond soup, 15

Chestnut and almond waffles with maple poached pears, 10

Endive and radicchio salad with apricots, toasted almonds and goat cheese, 102

Escarole, goat cheese, date and walnut salad with pomegranate dressing, 97

Flourless orange and almond cake, 118

Gevulde speculaas, 113

Green pea and cashew soup, 22

Malaysian-style vegetable and tofu curry, 52

Muhammara, 24

Mum's apricot nut bread, 109

Peanut sesame noodles, 99

Quinoa vegetable biryani, 85

Red lentil, sweet potato and peanut soup with greens, 22

Ricotta, orange and chocolate budino, 117

Roasted beet salad with beet greens, orzo, feta and pine nuts, 92

Spaghetti with roasted cauliflower, raisins, pine nuts and green olives, 46

Stuffed poblano makhani, 68

Tofu satay burger with caramelized onions and peanut sauce, 55

Walnut and mushroom pâté, 27

O

Oranges

Brazilian black bean and sweet potato soup with mango, 13

Fennel braised in orange juice, 88

Flourless orange and almond cake, 118

Ricotta, orange and chocolate budino, 117

Watercress, jicama and orange salad with cilantro-lime dressing, 101

P

Pancakes and Waffles

Chestnut and almond waffles with maple poached pears, 10

Swedish oatmeal pancakes with raspberry-cranberry compote, 2

Parsnips

Maple roasted parsnips, 90

Passion Fruit

Mango and passion fruit meringue roulade with raspberry sauce, 110

Pasta

Eggplant and lentil ragu, 38

Pasta e fagioli, 18

Roasted beet salad with beet greens, orzo pasta, feta and pine nuts, 92

Spaghetti with roasted cauliflower, raisins, pine nuts and green olives, 46

Strozzapreti with spinach sauce and sautéed mushrooms, 40

Pears

Arugula salad with sautéed mushrooms, pear, celery, walnuts and shaved parmesan, 97

Chestnut and almond waffles with maple poached pears, 10

Fresh ginger cakes with ginger crème anglaise and poached pear, 115

Pear, fresh ginger and date crumble, 112

Peas, green

Crostini with fresh pea and basil pesto, 24

Green pea and cashew soup, 22

Mini samosas with cilantro and mint chutney, 25

Quinoa salad with asparagus, fava beans, garden peas, mint and feta, 101

Quinoa vegetable biryani, 85

Peppers and Chilies
Late summer harvest vegetable tart, 47
Lentil and mushroom croquettes with roasted
 bell pepper gastrique, 76
Mexican tofu fajitas, 48
Muhammara, 24
Pan-fried ricotta polenta with ratatouille, 73
Peanut sesame noodles, 99
Portobello mushroom burgers with peperonata,
 arugula pesto and mozzarella, 54
Ratatouille masala, 90
Roasted bell pepper and carrot soup, 12
Roasted vegetable and cheese strudel with
 tomato coulis, 70
Sautéed sweet corn, zucchini and bell peppers
 with cilantro and lime, 89
Shakshouka, 5
Stuffed poblano makhani, 68
Vegetable and cannellini bean goulash with
 parsley dumplings, 60

Plums
Greta Anna's plum cake, 112
Prune flan, 111

Polenta
Grits with cheddar, spinach, tomato and
 poached eggs, 3
Pan-fried polenta with lemon, raisins, ricotta
 and maple syrup, 9
Pan-fried ricotta polenta with ratatouille, 73

Potatoes
Bubble and squeak with pan-fried tofu
 and onion gravy, 32
Curried potato and leek soup, 16
Mini samosas with cilantro and
 mint chutney, 25
Peruvian potato, cheese and avocado soup, 19
Potato roesti with sautéed mushrooms,
 poached eggs and sauce meurette, 72
Roasted potatoes pimentón, 82
Split pea and potato soup, 17
Stuffed poblano makhani, 68

Puddings and Flans
Apple bread and butter pudding, 107
Black sticky rice pudding with banana
 and coconut milk, 114
Prune flan, 111
Ricotta, orange and chocolate budino, 117

Pumpkin
See squash

Q

Quinoa
Quinoa salad with asparagus, fava, peas,
 mint and feta, 101
Quinoa pilaf, 84
Quinoa vegetable biryani, 85
Quinoa with roasted cauliflower and olives, 84

R
Raisins
Pan-fried polenta with lemon, raisins, ricotta
 and maple syrup, 9
Ricotta, orange and chocolate budino, 117

Rice
See Grains

Rhubarb
Rhubarb and buttermilk custard tart, 116

S
Salads
Arugula salad with sauteed mushrooms, pear,
 celery, walnuts and parmesan, 97
Arugula with grapes, almonds
 and manchego, 103
Baby spinach with roasted butternut squash
 and miso dressing, 92
Butter lettuce with avocado, mango,
 cucumber and chili-lime dressing, 93
Cold udon noodles with broccoli, tofu
 and pickled ginger dressing, 95

Endive and radicchio salad with apricots, goat cheese and almonds, 102

Escarole with goat cheese, dates, walnuts and pomegranate molasses, 97

Kale salad with pine nuts, currants and parmesan, 98

Peanut sesame noodles, 99

Quinoa salad with asparagus, fava, peas, mint and feta, 101

Roasted beet salad with beet greens, orzo, feta and pine nuts, 92

Watercress, jicama and orange salad with cilantro-lime dressing, 101

Sauces
Arugula pesto, 54
Besciamella, 64
Cilantro chutney, 7
Cilantro and mint chuntey, 25
Hoisin ginger sauce, 65
Makhani sauce, 68
Mushroom-rosemary au jus, 36
Peanut sauce, 55
Raspberry sauce, 110
Roasted bell pepper gastrique, 76
Sauce meurette, 72
Spinach sauce, 40
Tomato coulis, 70

Snow peas,
Peanut sesame noodles, 99

Soups
Brazilian black bean and sweet potato soup with mango, 13
Cannellini bean and kale, 14
Cauliflower and almond, 15
Curried potato and leek , 16
Green pea and cashew, 22
Pasta and fagioli with porcini mushrooms, 18
Peruvian potato, cheese and avocado, 19
Red lentil, sweet potato and peanut, 22
Roasted bell pepper and carrot, 12
Split pea and potato soup, 17
Yellow split pea and spinach dhal, 21

Sweet corn and miso, 16

Spinach
Baby spinach and roasted butternut squash salad with miso dressing, 92
Grits with cheddar, spinach, tomato and poached eggs, 3
Portobello mushrooms filled with caramelized onion, spinach, tomato and mozzarella, 43
Sautéed spinach with black mission figs, 83
Strozzapreti with spinach sauce and sautéed mushrooms, 40
Yellow split pea and spinach dhal, 21

Squash
Baby spinach and roasted butternut squash salad with miso dressing, 92
Butternut squash and ricotta galette with sage butter, 50
Pan-fried ricotta polenta with ratatouille, 73
Ratatouille masala, 90
Roasted vegetable and cheese strudel with tomato coulis, 70
Sautéed sweet corn, zucchini and bell peppers with cilantro and lime, 89

Sultanas
See Raisins

Sweet potatoes
Brazilian black bean and sweet potato soup with mango, 13
Bubble and squeak with pan-fried tofu and onion gravy, 32
Malaysian-style vegetable and tofu curry, 52
Red lentil, sweet potato and peanut soup with greens, 22
Sweet potato purée with stir-fried bok choy,
Sesame-crusted tofu and hoisin-ginger sauce, 65
Winter vegetable and miso stew, 56

ACKNOWLEDGMENTS

Thank you to the SYDA Foundation, where I received the bulk of my kitchen training and had the opportunity to refine my cooking skills, without which this book wouldn't exist.

A huge thank you to Miki Duisterhof for being so kind and generous, offering your time and experience to create the beautiful photos for this book. I am ever so grateful.

Thank you to Nan Whitney for offering your food styling expertise and props to many of the shots. A wonderful and unexpected gift.

Thank you to Junko Lowry for testing many of the recipes and whose love of food and cooking is so apparent. Your contribution was such an important ingredient in the refinement of my recipe development process.

Thank you to Dave Lieberman for editing my recipes. I feel very fortunate that you were recommended to me for this project.

Thank you to my brother Paul Tabak for spending many a late night at the computer working with me on the cover design, I hope I didn't drive you too crazy in the process!

Thank you to Auset Selassie for kindly offering your time to test recipes.

Thank you to Leonard Peters, my food critic/taster for many of the recipes I developed, offering valuable constructive feedback.

Thank you Lora Zarubin for generously offering the use of your props, which greatly enhanced the food shots.

Thank you to Sarah Forman for kindly sharing your tips and advice from your previous cookbook collaboration.

Thank you to my husband Leslie, who graciously put up with me spending a lot of time in the kitchen, testing and re-testing recipes.

Thank you to our sweet dog Luca, who unfailingly kept me company in the kitchen, albeit just to taste anything I was preparing.

all proceeds from the sale of this book go to the SYDA Foundation

ABOUT THE AUTHOR

Radha's love for cooking began at an early age. When most of her friends were reading fiction, Radha would be poring over cookbooks. She cooked in a number of vegetarian cafes in Sydney, Australia then over a period of nine years prepared vegetarian cuisine for an international foundation in Australia, India and the U.S.A. In addition, she trained in several healing modalities including nutrition and herbal medicine. Radha currently lives in New York City where she has worked as a personal chef since 2008, cooking personalized meals for her clients.

Made in the USA
Columbia, SC
31 January 2018